COLLINS

SPAN
VERB TA
AND GRA

D0441513

COLLINS GEM

SPANISH
VERB TABLES
AND GRAMMAR

Collins Gem

An imprint of HarperCollins*Publishers*

First published in this edition 1995

© HarperCollins Publishers 1995

latest reprint 1999

ISBN 0 00 471001-0 Paperback

Collins Gem ® is a registered trademark of
HarperCollins Publishers Limited

A de Benito de Harland
In consultation with
I F Ariza

editor
Jeremy Butterfield

editorial staff
Linda Chestnutt
Enrique González Sardinero

editorial management
Vivian Marr

---

*A catalogue record for this book
is available from the British Library*

*Typeset by Morton Word Processing Ltd,
Scarborough*

*Printed and bound in Great Britain by
Caledonian International Book Manufacturing Ltd,
Glasgow, G64*

Your **Collins Gem Spanish Verb Tables and Grammar** is designed to offer students of Spanish of all ages and at all levels an uncluttered, step-by-step guide to the grammar of the language. For beginners, the book provides a clear introduction to all the basic rules and structures, and more advanced learners will find it an invaluable guide for reference and revision.

For ease of use, each part of speech (nouns, verbs, adjectives etc) has been treated separately (see the list of contents on the next page).

A special feature of this book is the clear demarcation of grammatical points, each treated on a left-hand page, and illustrated by examples in up-to-date Spanish on the opposite right-hand page. The appropriate example is clearly indicated by a system of bracketed numbers e.g. (→**1**), (→**2**) etc, corresponding to an example number on the facing page.

Special attention has been paid throughout to areas in which Spanish and English usage differ, thus helping the user to avoid the mistake of trying to translate English structures by identical structures in Spanish.

The tables of irregular verbs complement the extensive treatment of regular verbs in the grammar section of the book. In them 80 major irregular verbs are conjugated in their simple tenses so you can see where they differ from regular verbs. In addition, the verb index, in which all verbs are cross-referred to the appropriate conjugation model, enables you to check how over 2,800 Spanish verbs are conjugated.

A comprehensive index, containing key words in both Spanish and English, as well as subject references, completes the grammar.

Abbreviations used

algn	alguien	**masc**	masculine	**pres**	present
cond	conditional	**p(p)**	page(s)	**sb**	somebody
contd	continued	**perf**	perfect	**sing**	singular
fem	feminine	**pluperf**	pluperfect	**sth**	something
infin	infinitive	**plur**	plural	**subj**	subjunctive

4 CONTENTS

6 VERBS

Simple Tenses: Formation

In Spanish the simple tenses are:

Present	(→**1**)
Imperfect	(→**2**)
Future	(→**3**)
Conditional	(→**4**)
Preterite	(→**5**)
Present Subjunctive	(→**6**)
Imperfect Subjunctive	(→**7**)

They are formed by adding endings to a verb stem. The endings show the number and person of the subject of the verb. (→**8**)

The stem and endings of regular verbs are totally predictable. The following sections show all the patterns for regular verbs. For irregular verbs see pp 80 ff.

Regular Verbs

There are three regular verb patterns (called conjugations), each identifiable by the ending of the infinitive:

- First conjugation verbs end in -**ar** e.g. **hablar** to speak

- Second conjugation verbs end in -**er** e.g. **comer** to eat

- Third conjugation verbs end in -**ir** e.g. **vivir** to live

These three conjugations are treated in order on the following pages. The subject pronouns will appear in brackets because they are not always necessary in Spanish (see p 226).

Continued

1 (yo) hablo
I speak, I am speaking, I do speak

2 (yo) hablaba
I spoke, I was speaking, I used to speak

3 (yo) hablaré
I shall speak, I shall be speaking

4 (yo) hablaría
I should/would speak, I should/would be speaking

5 (yo) hablé
I spoke

6 (que) (yo) hable
(that) I speak

7 (que) (yo) hablara *or* **hablase**
(that) I speak

8 (yo) hablo   I speak
   (nosotros) hablamos   we speak
   (yo) hablaría   I would speak
   (nosotros) hablaríamos   we would speak

Simple Tenses: First Conjugation

- The stem is formed as follows:

TENSE	FORMATION	EXAMPLE
Present		
Imperfect		
Preterite	infinitive minus -ar	habl-
Present Subjunctive		
Imperfect Subjunctive*	* For irregular verbs see p 80	
Future	infinitive	hablar-
Conditional		

- To the appropriate stem add the following endings:

		PRESENT (→1)	IMPERFECT (→2)	PRETERITE (→3)
sing	1st person	-o	-aba	-é
	2nd person	-as	-abas	-aste
	3rd person	-a	-aba	-ó
plur	1st person	-amos	-ábamos	-amos
	2nd person	-áis	-abais	-asteis
	3rd person	-an	-aban	-aron

		PRESENT SUBJUNCTIVE (→4)	IMPERFECT SUBJUNCTIVE (→5)
sing	1st person	-e	-ara or -ase
	2nd person	-es	-aras or -ases
	3rd person	-e	-ara or -ase
plur	1st person	-emos	-áramos or -ásemos
	2nd person	-éis	-arais or -aseis
	3rd person	-en	-aran or -asen

		FUTURE (→6)	CONDITIONAL (→7)
sing	1st person	-é	-ía
	2nd person	-ás	-ías
	3rd person	-á	-ía
plur	1st person	-emos	-íamos
	2nd person	-éis	-íais
	3rd person	-án	-ían

1 *PRESENT*   **2** *IMPERFECT*   **3** *PRETERITE*

(yo)	hablo	hablaba	hablé
(tú)	hablas	hablabas	hablaste
(él/ella/Vd)	habla	hablaba	habló
(nosotros/as)	hablamos	hablábamos	hablamos
(vosotros/as)	habláis	hablabais	hablasteis
(ellos/as/Vds)	hablan	hablaban	hablaron

4 *PRESENT SUBJUNCTIVE*   **5** *IMPERFECT SUBJUNCTIVE*

(yo)	hable	hablara or hablase
(tú)	hables	hablaras or hablases
(él/ella/Vd)	hable	hablara or hablase
(nosotros/as)	hablemos	habláramos or hablásemos
(vosotros/as)	habléis	hablarais or hablaseis
(ellos/as/Vds)	hablen	hablaran or hablasen

6 *FUTURE*   **7** *CONDITIONAL*

(yo)	hablaré	hablaría
(tú)	hablarás	hablarías
(él/ella/Vd)	hablará	hablaría
(nosotros/as)	hablaremos	hablaríamos
(vosotros/as)	hablaréis	hablaríais
(ellos/as/Vds)	hablarán	hablarían

Simple Tenses: Second Conjugation

- The stem is formed as follows:

TENSE	FORMATION	EXAMPLE
Present		
Imperfect		
Preterite	infinitive minus -er	com-
Present Subjunctive		
Imperfect Subjunctive*	* For irregular verbs see p 80	
Future	infinitive	comer-
Conditional		

- To the appropriate stem add the following endings:

		PRESENT (→1)	IMPERFECT (→2)	PRETERITE (→3)
sing	1st person	-o	-ía	-í
	2nd person	-es	-ías	-iste
	3rd person	-e	-ía	-ió
plur	1st person	-emos	-íamos	-imos
	2nd person	-éis	-íais	-isteis
	3rd person	-en	-ían	-ieron

		PRESENT SUBJUNCTIVE (→4)	IMPERFECT SUBJUNCTIVE (→5)
sing	1st person	-a	-iera or -iese
	2nd person	-as	-ieras or -ieses
	3rd person	-a	-iera or -iese
plur	1st person	-amos	-iéramos or -iésemos
	2nd person	-áis	-ierais or -ieseis
	3rd person	-an	-ieran or -iesen

		FUTURE (→6)	CONDITIONAL (→7)
sing	1st person	-é	-ía
	2nd person	-ás	-ías
	3rd person	-á	-ía
plur	1st person	-emos	-íamos
	2nd person	-éis	-íais
	3rd person	-án	-ían

1 *PRESENT*

(yo)	como
(tú)	comes
(él/ella/Vd)	come
(nosotros/as)	comemos
(vosotros/as)	coméis
(ellos/as/Vds)	comen

2 *IMPERFECT*

comía
comías
comía
comíamos
comíais
comían

3 *PRETERITE*

comí
comiste
comió
comimos
comisteis
comieron

4 *PRESENT SUBJUNCTIVE*

(yo)	coma
(tú)	comas
(él/ella/Vd)	coma
(nosotros/as)	comamos
(vosotros/as)	comáis
(ellos/as/Vds)	coman

5 *IMPERFECT SUBJUNCTIVE*

comiera *or* comiese
comieras *or* comieses
comiera *or* comiese
comiéramos *or* comiésemos
comierais *or* comieseis
comieran *or* comiesen

6 *FUTURE*

(yo)	comeré
(tú)	comerás
(él/ella/Vd)	comerá
(nosotros/as)	comeremos
(vosotros/as)	comeréis
(ellos/as/Vds)	comerán

7 *CONDITIONAL*

comería
comerías
comería
comeríamos
comeríais
comerían

Simple Tenses: Third Conjugation

● The stem is formed as follows:

TENSE	FORMATION	EXAMPLE
Present		
Imperfect		
Preterite	infinitive minus -ir	viv-
Present Subjunctive		
Imperfect Subjunctive*	* For irregular verbs see p 80	
Future	infinitive	vivir-
Conditional		

● To the appropriate stem add the following endings:

		PRESENT (→1)	IMPERFECT (→2)	PRETERITE (→3)
sing	1st person	-o	-ía	-í
	2nd person	-es	-ías	-iste
	3rd person	-e	-ía	-ió
plur	1st person	-imos	-íamos	-imos
	2nd person	-ís	-íais	-isteis
	3rd person	-en	-ían	-ieron

		PRESENT SUBJUNCTIVE (→4)	IMPERFECT SUBJUNCTIVE (→5)
sing	1st person	-a	-iera or -iese
	2nd person	-as	-ieras or -ieses
	3rd person	-a	-iera or -iese
plur	1st person	-amos	-iéramos or -iésemos
	2nd person	-áis	-ierais or -ieseis
	3rd person	-an	-ieran or -iesen

		FUTURE (→6)	CONDITIONAL (→7)
sing	1st person	-é	-ía
	2nd person	-ás	-ías
	3rd person	-á	-ía
plur	1st person	-emos	-íamos
	2nd person	-éis	-íais
	3rd person	-án	-ían

1 *PRESENT*   **2** *IMPERFECT*   **3** *PRETERITE*

(yo)	vivo	vivía	viví
(tú)	vives	vivías	viviste
(él/ella/Vd)	vive	vivía	vivió
(nosotros/as)	vivimos	vivíamos	vivimos
(vosotros/as)	vivís	vivíais	vivisteis
(ellos/as/Vds)	viven	vivían	vivieron

4 *PRESENT SUBJUNCTIVE*   **5** *IMPERFECT SUBJUNCTIVE*

(yo)	viva	viviera *or* viviese
(tú)	vivas	vivieras *or* vivieses
(él/ella/Vd)	viva	viviera *or* viviese
(nosotros/as)	vivamos	viviéramos *or* viviésemos
(vosotros/as)	viváis	vivierais *or* vivieseis
(ellos/as/Vds)	vivan	vivieran *or* viviesen

6 *FUTURE*   **7** *CONDITIONAL*

(yo)	viviré	viviría
(tú)	vivirás	vivirías
(él/ella/Vd)	vivirá	viviría
(nosotros/as)	viviremos	viviríamos
(vosotros/as)	viviréis	viviríais
(ellos/as/Vds)	vivirán	vivirían

The Imperative

The imperative is the form of the verb used to give commands or orders. It can be used politely, as in English 'Shut the door, please'.

In POSITIVE commands, the imperative forms for **Vd**, **Vds** and **nosotros** are the same as the subjunctive. The other forms are as follows:

> **tú** (same as 3rd person singular present indicative)
> **vosotros** (final **-r** of infinitive changes to **-d**) (→1)

(tú)	**habla**	**come**	**vive**
	speak	*eat*	*live*
(Vd)	**hable**	**coma**	**viva**
	speak	*eat*	*live*
(nosotros)	**hablemos**	**comamos**	**vivamos**
	let's speak	*let's eat*	*let's live*
(vosotros)	**hablad**	**comed**	**vivid**
	speak	*eat*	*live*
(Vds)	**hablen**	**coman**	**vivan**
	speak	*eat*	*live*

In NEGATIVE commands, all the imperative forms are exactly the same as the present subjunctive.

• The imperative of irregular verbs is given in the verb tables, pp 82 ff.

Position of object pronouns with the imperative

In POSITIVE commands: they follow the verb and are attached to it. An accent is needed to show the correct position for stress (see p 292) (→2)
In NEGATIVE commands: they precede the verb and are not attached to it (→3)

• For the order of object pronouns, see page 232.

Continued

1 cantar
to sing

cantad
sing

2 Perdóneme
Excuse me
Elíjanos
Choose us
Esperémosla
Let's wait for her/it

Enviémoselos
Let's send them to him/her/them
Explíquemelo
Explain it to me
Devuélvaselo
Give it back to him/her/them

3 No me molestes
Don't disturb me

No les castiguemos
Let's not punish them
No las conteste
Don't answer them

No se la devolvamos
Let's not give it back to him/her/
them
No me lo mandes
Don't send it to me
No nos lo hagan
Don't do it to us

The Imperative (contd)

- For reflexive verbs – e.g. **levantarse** *to get up* – the object pronoun is the reflexive pronoun. It should be noted that the imperative forms need an accent to show the correct position for stress (see p 292). The forms **nosotros** and **vosotros** also drop the final **-s** and **-d** respectively before the pronoun (→1)

  EXCEPTION: **idos (vosotros)** *go*

- Note: For general instructions, the infinitive is used instead of the imperative (→2), but when it is preceded by **vamos a** it often translates *let's* … (→3)

1 Levántate
Get up
Levántese (Vd)
Get up
Levantémonos
Let's get up
Levantaos
Get up
Levántense (Vds)
Get up

No te levantes
Don't get up
No se levante (Vd)
Don't get up
No nos levantemos
Let's not get up
No os levantéis
Don't get up
No se levanten (Vds)
Don't get up

2 Ver pág ...
See page ...
No pasar
Do not pass

3 Vamos a ver
Let's see
Vamos a empezar
Let's start

18   VERBS

Compound Tenses: Formation

In Spanish the compound tenses are:

Perfect	(→**1**)
Pluperfect	(→**2**)
Future Perfect	(→**3**)
Conditional Perfect	(→**4**)
Past Anterior	(→**5**)
Perfect Subjunctive	(→**6**)
Pluperfect Subjunctive	(→**7**)

They consist of the past participle of the verb together with the auxiliary verb **haber**.

Compound tenses are formed in exactly the same way for both regular and irregular verbs, the only difference being that irregular verbs may have an irregular past participle.

The Past Participle

For all compound tenses you need to know how to form the past participle of the verb. For regular verbs this is as follows:

- 1st conjugation: replace the **-ar** of the infinitive by **-ado** (→**8**)

- 2nd conjugation: replace the **-er** of the infinitive by **-ido** (→**9**)

- 3rd conjugation: replace the **-ir** of the infinitive by **-ido** (→**10**)

Continued

1 (yo) he hablado
I have spoken

2 (yo) había hablado
I had spoken

3 (yo) habré hablado
I shall have spoken

4 (yo) habría hablado
I should/would have spoken

5 (yo) hube hablado
I had spoken

6 (que) (yo) haya hablado
(that) I spoke, have spoken

7 (que) (yo) hubiera/hubiese hablado
(that) I had spoken

8 cantar   →   cantado
  to sing   sung

9 comer   →   comido
  to eat   eaten

10 vivir   →   vivido
  to live   lived

Compound Tenses: formation (contd)

Perfect tense:	the present tense of **haber** plus the past participle (→1)
Pluperfect tense:	the imperfect tense of **haber** plus the past participle (→2)
Future Perfect:	the future tense of **haber** plus the past participle (→3)
Conditional Perfect:	the conditional of **haber** plus the past participle (→4)

Continued

1 *PERFECT*

(yo)	**he** hablado
(tú)	**has** hablado
(él/ella/Vd)	**ha** hablado
(nosotros/as)	**hemos** hablado
(vosotros/as)	**habéis** hablado
(ellos/as/Vds)	**han** hablado

2 *PLUPERFECT*

(yo)	**había** hablado
(tú)	**habías** hablado
(él/ella/Vd)	**había** hablado
(nosotros/as)	**habíamos** hablado
(vosotros/as)	**habíais** hablado
(ellos/as/Vds)	**habían** hablado

3 *FUTURE PERFECT*

(yo)	**habré** hablado
(tú)	**habrás** hablado
(él/ella/Vd)	**habrá** hablado
(nosotros/as)	**habremos** hablado
(vosotros/as)	**habréis** hablado
(ellos/as/Vds)	**habrán** hablado

4 *CONDITIONAL PERFECT*

(yo)	**habría** hablado
(tú)	**habrías** hablado
(él/ella/Vd)	**habría** hablado
(nosotros/as)	**habríamos** hablado
(vosotros/as)	**habríais** hablado
(ellos/as/Vds)	**habrían** hablado

Compound Tenses: formation (contd)

Past Anterior: the preterite of **haber** plus the past
                            participle (→**1**)

Perfect Subjunctive: the present subjunctive of **haber** plus
                            the past participle (→**2**)

Pluperfect Subjunctive: the imperfect subjunctive of **haber** plus
                            the past participle (→**3**)

• For how to form the past participle of regular verbs see p 18.
The past participle of irregular verbs is given for each verb in
the verb tables, pp 82 to 161.

1 *PAST ANTERIOR*

(yo)	**hube** hablado
(tú)	**hubiste** hablado
(él/ella/Vd)	**hubo** hablado
(nosotros/as)	**hubimos** hablado
(vosotros/as)	**hubisteis** hablado
(ellos/as/Vds)	**hubieron** hablado

2 *PRESENT SUBJUNCTIVE*

(yo)	**haya** hablado
(tú)	**hayas** hablado
(él/ella/Vd)	**haya** hablado
(nosotros/as)	**hayamos** hablado
(vosotros/as)	**hayáis** hablado
(ellos/as/Vds)	**hayan** hablado

3 *PLUPERFECT SUBJUNCTIVE*

(yo)	**hubiera** or **hubiese** hablado
(tú)	**hubieras** or **hubieses** hablado
(él/ella/Vd)	**hubiera** or **hubiese** hablado
(nosotros/as)	**hubiéramos** or **hubiésemos** hablado
(vosotros/as)	**hubierais** or **hubieseis** hablado
(ellos/as/Vds)	**hubieran** or **hubiesen** hablado

Reflexive Verbs

A reflexive verb is one accompanied by a reflexive pronoun. The infinitive of a reflexive verb ends with the pronoun **se**, which is added to the verb form e.g.
levantarse *to get up*; **lavarse** *to wash (oneself)*.

The reflexive pronouns are:

PERSON	SINGULAR	PLURAL
1st	**me**	**nos**
2nd	**te**	**os**
3rd	**se**	**se**

- The reflexive pronoun 'reflects back' to the subject, but it is not always translated in English (→**1**)
  The plural pronouns are sometimes translated as *one another, each other* (the 'reciprocal' meaning) (→**2**)
  The reciprocal meaning may be emphasized by **el uno al otro/la una a la otra (los unos a los otros/las unas a las otras)** (→**3**)

- Both simple and compound tenses of reflexive verbs are conjugated in exactly the same way as those of non-reflexive verbs, except that the reflexive pronoun is always used.
  The only irregularity is in the 1st and 2nd person plural of the affirmative imperative (see p 16). A sample reflexive verb is conjugated in full on pp 28 to 31.

Position of reflexive pronouns

- Except with the infinitive, gerund and positive commands, the pronoun comes before the verb (→**4**)

- In the infinitive, gerund and positive commands, the pronoun follows the verb and is attached to it (but see also p 228) (→**5**)

Continued

1 Me visto
I'm dressing (myself)
Nos lavamos
We're washing (ourselves)
Se levanta
He gets up

2 Nos queremos
We love each other
Se parecen
They resemble one another

3 Se miraban el uno al otro
They were looking at each other

4 Me acuesto temprano
I go to bed early
¿Cómo se llama Vd?
What is your name?
No se ha despertado
He hasn't woken up
No te levantes
Don't get up

5 Quiero irme
I want to go away
Estoy levantándome
I am getting up
Siéntense
Sit down
Vámonos
Let's go

Reflexive Verbs (contd)

Some verbs have both a reflexive and non-reflexive form. When used reflexively, they have a different but closely related meaning, as shown in the following examples.

NON-REFLEXIVE	*REFLEXIVE*
acostar to put to bed	**acostarse** to go to bed
casar to marry (off)	**casarse** to get married
detener to stop	**detenerse** to come to a halt
dormir to sleep	**dormirse** to go to sleep
enfadar to annoy	**enfadarse** to get annoyed
hacer to make	**hacerse** to become
ir to go	**irse** to leave, go away
lavar to wash	**lavarse** to get washed
levantar to raise	**levantarse** to get up
llamar to call	**llamarse** to be called
poner to put	**ponerse** to put on (clothing), to become
sentir to feel (something)	**sentirse** to feel (sick, tired, etc)
vestir to dress (someone)	**vestirse** to get dressed
volver to return	**volverse** to turn round

● Some other verbs exist only in the reflexive:

arrepentirse to repent	**jactarse** to boast
atreverse to dare	**quejarse** to complain

● Some verbs acquire a different nuance when used reflexively:

caer to fall (→1)	**caerse** to fall down (by accident) (→2)
morir to die, be killed (by accident or on purpose) (→3)	**morirse** to die (from natural causes) (→4)

● Often a reflexive verb can be used:
  – to avoid the passive (see p 34) (→5)
  – in impersonal expressions (see p 40) (→6)

Continued

1 El agua caía desde las rocas
Water fell from the rocks

2 Me caí y me rompí el brazo
I fell and broke my arm

3 Tres personas han muerto en un accidente/atentado terrorista
Three people were killed in an accident/a terrorist attack

4 Mi abuelo se murió a los ochenta años
My grandfather died at the age of eighty

5 Se perdió la batalla
The battle was lost
No se veían las casas
The houses could not be seen

6 Se dice que ...
(It is said that) People say that ...
No se puede entrar
You/One can't go in
No se permite
It is not allowed

Reflexive Verbs (contd)

Conjugation of: **lavarse** *to wash oneself*

I *SIMPLE TENSES*

PRESENT

(yo)	**me lavo**
(tú)	**te lavas**
(él/ella/Vd)	**se lava**
(nosotros/as)	**nos lavamos**
(vosotros/as)	**os laváis**
(ellos/as/Vds)	**se lavan**

IMPERFECT

(yo)	**me lavaba**
(tú)	**te lavabas**
(él/ella/Vd)	**se lavaba**
(nosotros/as)	**nos lavábamos**
(vosotros/as)	**os lavabais**
(ellos/as/Vds)	**se lavaban**

FUTURE

(yo)	**me lavaré**
(tú)	**te lavarás**
(él/ella/Vd)	**se lavará**
(nosotros/as)	**nos lavaremos**
(vosotros/as)	**os lavaréis**
(ellos/as/Vds)	**se lavarán**

CONDITIONAL

(yo)	**me lavaría**
(tú)	**te lavarías**
(él/ella/Vd)	**se lavaría**
(nosotros/as)	**nos lavaríamos**
(vosotros/as)	**os lavaríais**
(ellos/as/Vds)	**se lavarían**

Reflexive Verbs (contd)

Conjugation of: **lavarse** to wash oneself

I *SIMPLE TENSES*

PRETERITE

(yo)	**me** lav**é**
(tú)	**te** lav**aste**
(él/ella/Vd)	**se** lav**ó**
(nosotros/as)	**nos** lav**amos**
(vosotros/as)	**os** lav**asteis**
(ellos/as/Vds)	**se** lav**aron**

PRESENT SUBJUNCTIVE

(yo)	**me** lav**e**
(tú)	**te** lav**es**
(él/ella/Vd)	**se** lav**e**
(nosotros/as)	**nos** lav**emos**
(vosotros/as)	**os** lav**éis**
(ellos/as/Vds)	**se** lav**en**

IMPERFECT SUBJUNCTIVE

(yo)	**me** lav**ara** *or* lav**ase**
(tú)	**te** lav**aras** *or* lav**ases**
(él/ella/Vd)	**se** lav**ara** *or* lav**ase**
(nosotros/as)	**nos** lav**áramos** *or* lav**ásemos**
(vosotros/as)	**os** lav**arais** *or* lav**aseis**
(ellos/as/Vds)	**se** lav**aran** *or* lav**asen**

Continued

Reflexive Verbs (contd)

Conjugation of: **lavarse** *to wash oneself*

II *COMPOUND TENSES*

PERFECT

(yo)	**me he** lavado
(tú)	**te has** lavado
(él/ella/Vd)	**se ha** lavado
(nosotros/as)	**nos hemos** lavado
(vosotros/as)	**os habéis** lavado
(ellos/as/Vds)	**se han** lavado

PLUPERFECT

(yo)	**me había** lavado
(tú)	**te habías** lavado
(él/ella/Vd)	**se había** lavado
(nosotros/as)	**nos habíamos** lavado
(vosotros/as)	**os habíais** lavado
(ellos/as/Vds)	**se habían** lavado

FUTURE PERFECT

(yo)	**me habré** lavado
(tú)	**te habrás** lavado
(él/ella/Vd)	**se habrá** lavado
(nosotros/as)	**nos habremos** lavado
(vosotros/as)	**os habréis** lavado
(ellos/as/Vds)	**se habrán** lavado

Reflexive Verbs (contd)

Conjugation of: **lavarse** *to wash oneself*

II *COMPOUND TENSES*

PAST ANTERIOR

(yo)	**me hube** lavado
(tú)	**te hubiste** lavado
(él/ella/Vd)	**se hubo** lavado
(nosotros/as)	**nos hubimos** lavado
(vosotros/as)	**os hubisteis** lavado
(ellos/as/Vds)	**se hubieron** lavado

PERFECT SUBJUNCTIVE

(yo)	**me haya** lavado
(tú)	**te hayas** lavado
(él/ella/Vd)	**se haya** lavado
(nosotros/as)	**nos hayamos** lavado
(vosotros/as)	**os hayáis** lavado
(ellos/as/Vds)	**se hayan** lavado

PLUPERFECT SUBJUNCTIVE

(yo)	**me hubiera** *or* **hubiese** lavado
(tú)	**te hubieras** *or* **hubieses** lavado
(él/ella/Vd)	**se hubiera** *or* **hubiese** lavado
(nosotros/as)	**nos hubiéramos** *or* **hubiésemos** lavado
(vosotros/as)	**os hubierais** *or* **hubieseis** lavado
(ellos/as/Vds)	**se hubieran** *or* **hubiesen** lavado

The Passive

In active sentences, the subject of a verb carries out the action of
that verb, but in passive sentences the subject receives the action.
Compare the following:

The car hit Jane (subject: *the car*)
Jane was hit by the car (subject: *Jane*)

- English uses the verb '*to be*' with the past participle to form
  passive sentences. Spanish forms them in the same way, i.e.:
    a tense of **ser** + past participle
  The past participle agrees in number and gender with the
  subject (→1)

  A sample verb is conjugated in the passive voice on pp 36 to 39.

- In English, the word '*by*' usually introduces the agent through
  which the action of a passive sentence is performed. In Spanish
  this agent is preceded by **por** (→2)

- The Passive voice is used much less frequently in Spanish than
  English. It is, however, often used in expressions where the
  identity of the agent is unknown or unimportant (→3)

Continued

1 Pablo ha sido despedido
Paul has been sacked
Su madre era muy admirada
His mother was greatly admired
El palacio será vendido
The palace will be sold
Las puertas habían sido cerradas
The doors had been closed

2 La casa fue diseñada por mi hermano
The house was designed by my brother

3 La ciudad fue conquistada tras un largo asedio
The city was conquered after a long siege
Ha sido declarado el estado de excepción
A state of emergency has been declared

The Passive (contd)

In English the indirect object in an active sentence can become the subject of the related passive sentence,
e.g. *His mother gave him the book* (indirect object: *him*)
    He was given the book by his mother

This is not possible in Spanish. The indirect object remains as such, while the object of the active sentence becomes the subject of the passive sentence (→**1**)

Other ways to express a passive meaning

Since modern Spanish tends to avoid the passive, it uses various other constructions to replace it:

- If the agent (person or object performing the action) is known, the active is often preferred where English might prefer the passive (→**2**)

- The 3rd person plural of the active voice can be used. The meaning is equivalent to *they* + verb (→**3**)

- When the action of the sentence is performed on a person, the reflexive form of the verb can be used in the 3rd person singular, and the person becomes the object (→**4**)

- When the action is performed on a thing, this becomes the subject of the sentence and the verb is made reflexive, agreeing in number with the subject (→**5**)

Continued

1 **Su madre le regaló el libro**
  His mother gave him the book
  becomes
  El libro le fue regalado por su madre
  The book was given to him by his mother

2 **La policía interrogó al sospechoso**
  The police questioned the suspect
  rather than
  El sospechoso fue interrogado por la policía

3 **Usan demasiada publicidad en la televisión**
  Too much advertising is used on television

4 **Últimamente no se le/les ha visto mucho en público**
  He has/they have not been seen much in public recently

5 **Esta palabra ya no se usa**
  This word is no longer used
  Todos los libros se han vendido
  All the books have been sold

The Passive (contd)

Conjugation of: **ser amado** *to be loved*

PRESENT

(yo)	**soy** amado(a)
(tú)	**eres** amado(a)
(él/ella/Vd)	**es** amado(a)
(nosotros/as)	**somos** amado(a)s
(vosotros/as)	**sois** amado(a)s
(ellos/as/Vds)	**son** amado(a)s

IMPERFECT

(yo)	**era** amado(a)
(tú)	**eras** amado(a)
(él/ella/Vd)	**era** amado(a)
(nosotros/as)	**éramos** amado(a)s
(vosotros/as)	**erais** amado(a)s
(ellos/as/Vds)	**eran** amado(a)s

FUTURE

(yo)	**seré** amado(a)
(tú)	**serás** amado(a)
(él/ella/Vd)	**será** amado(a)
(nosotros/as)	**seremos** amado(a)s
(vosotros/as)	**seréis** amado(a)s
(ellos/as/Vds)	**serán** amado(a)s

CONDITIONAL

(yo)	**sería** amado(a)
(tú)	**serías** amado(a)
(él/ella/Vd)	**sería** amado(a)
(nosotros/as)	**seríamos** amado(a)s
(vosotros/as)	**seríais** amado(a)s
(ellos/as/Vds)	**serían** amado(a)s

The Passive (contd)

Conjugation of: **ser amado** *to be loved*

PRETERITE

(yo)	**fui** amado(a)
(tú)	**fuiste** amado(a)
(él/ella/Vd)	**fue** amado(a)
(nosotros/as)	**fuimos** amado(a)s
(vosotros/as)	**fuisteis** amado(a)s
(ellos/as/Vds)	**fueron** amado(a)s

PRESENT SUBJUNCTIVE

(yo)	**sea** amado(a)
(tú)	**seas** amado(a)
(él/ella/Vd)	**sea** amado(a)
(nosotros/as)	**seamos** amado(a)s
(vosotros/as)	**seáis** amado(a)s
(ellos/as/Vds)	**sean** amado(a)s

IMPERFECT SUBJUNCTIVE

(yo)	**fuera** *or* **fuese** amado(a)
(tú)	**fueras** *or* **fueses** amado(a)
(él/ella/Vd)	**fuera** *or* **fuese** amado(a)
(nosotros/as)	**fuéramos** *or* **fuésemos** amado(a)s
(vosotros/as)	**fuerais** *or* **fueseis** amado(a)s
(ellos/as/Vds)	**fueran** *or* **fuesen** amado(a)s

Continued

The Passive (contd)

Conjugation of: **ser amado** *to be loved*

PERFECT

(yo)	**he sido** amado(a)
(tú)	**has sido** amado(a)
(él/ella/Vd)	**ha sido** amado(a)
(nosotros/as)	**hemos sido** amado(a)s
(vosotros/as)	**habéis sido** amado(a)s
(ellos/as/Vds)	**han sido** amado(a)s

PLUPERFECT

(yo)	**había sido** amado(a)
(tú)	**habías sido** amado(a)
(él/ella/Vd)	**había sido** amado(a)
(nosotros/as)	**habíamos sido** amado(a)s
(vosotros/as)	**habíais sido** amado(a)s
(ellos/as/Vds)	**habían sido** amado(a)s

FUTURE PERFECT

(yo)	**habré sido** amado(a)
(tú)	**habrás sido** amado(a)
(él/ella/Vd)	**habrá sido** amado(a)
(nosotros/as)	**habremos sido** amado(a)s
(vosotros/as)	**habréis sido** amado(a)s
(ellos/as/Vds)	**habrán sido** amado(a)s

CONDITIONAL PERFECT

(yo)	**habría sido** amado(a)
(tú)	**habrías sido** amado(a)
(él/ella/Vd)	**habría sido** amado(a)
(nosotros/as)	**habríamos sido** amado(a)s
(vosotros/as)	**habríais sido** amado(a)s
(ellos/as/Vds)	**habrían sido** amado(a)s

The Passive (contd)

Conjugation of: **ser amado** *to be loved*

PAST ANTERIOR

(yo)	**hube sido** amado(a)
(tú)	**hubiste sido** amado(a)
(él/ella/Vd)	**hubo sido** amado(a)
(nosotros/as)	**hubimos sido** amado(a)s
(vosotros/as)	**hubisteis sido** amado(a)s
(ellos/as/Vds)	**hubieron sido** amado(a)s

PERFECT SUBJUNCTIVE

(yo)	**haya sido** amado(a)
(tú)	**hayas sido** amado(a)
(él/ella/Vd)	**haya sido** amado(a)
(nosotros/as)	**hayamos sido** amado(a)s
(vosotros/as)	**hayáis sido** amado(a)s
(ellos/as/Vds)	**hayan sido** amado(a)s

PLUPERFECT SUBJUNCTIVE

(yo)	**hubiera/-se sido** amado(a)
(tú)	**hubieras/-ses sido** amado(a)
(él/ella/Vd)	**hubiera/-se sido** amado(a)
(nosotros/as)	**hubiéramos/-semos sido** amado(a)s
(vosotros/as)	**hubierais/-seis sido** amado(a)s
(ellos/as/Vds)	**hubieran/-sen sido** amado(a)s

Impersonal Verbs

Impersonal verbs are used only in the infinitive, the gerund, and in the 3rd person (usually singular); unlike English, Spanish does not use the subject pronoun with impersonal verbs.

e.g. **llueve**
it's raining
es fácil decir que ...
it's easy to say that ...

The most common impersonal verbs are:

INFINITIVE	CONSTRUCTION	
amanecer	**amanece/está amaneciendo** *it's daybreak*	
anochecer	**anochece/está anocheciendo** *it's getting dark*	
granizar	**graniza/está granizando** *it's hailing*	
llover	**llueve/está lloviendo** *it's raining*	(→1)
lloviznar	**llovizna/está lloviznando** *it's drizzling*	
nevar	**nieva/está nevando** *it's snowing*	
tronar	**truena/está tronando** *it's thundering*	

Some reflexive verbs are also used impersonally.
The most common are:

INFINITIVE	CONSTRUCTION
creerse	**se cree que*** + indicative (→2) *it is thought that; people think that*
decirse	**se dice que*** + indicative (→3) *it is said that; people say that*

Continued

1 Llovía a cántaros
It was raining cats and dogs
Estaba nevando cuando salieron
It was snowing when they left

2 Se cree que llegarán mañana
It is thought they will arrive tomorrow

3 Se dice que ha sido el peor invierno en 50 años
People say it's been the worst winter in 50 years

42 VERBS

Impersonal Verbs (contd)

INFINITIVE	CONSTRUCTION
poderse	**se puede** + infinitive (→1)
	one/people can, it is possible to
tratarse de	**se trata de** + noun (→2)
	it's a question/matter of something
	it's about something
	se trata de + infinitive (→3)
	it's a question/matter of doing; somebody must do
venderse	**se vende*** + noun (→4)
	to be sold; for sale

*This impersonal construction conveys the same meaning as the 3rd person plural of these verbs; **creen que, dicen que, venden**

The following verbs are also commonly used in impersonal contructions:

INFINITIVE	CONSTRUCTION
bastar	**basta con** + infinitive (→5)
	it is enough to do
	basta con + noun (→6)
	something is enough, it only takes sth
faltar	**falta** + infinitive (→7)
	we still have to/one still has to
haber	**hay** + noun (→8)
	there is/are
	hay que + infinitive (→9)
	one has to/we have to
hacer	**hace** + noun/adjective depicting weather/dark/light etc (→10)
	it is
	hace + time expression + **que** + indicative (→11)
	somebody has done or been doing something since …
	hace + time expression + **que** + negative indicative (→12)
	it is … since

Continued

1 Aquí se puede aparcar
One can park here

2 No se trata de dinero
It isn't a question/matter of money

3 Se trata de poner fin al asunto
We must put an end to the matter

4 Se vende coche
Car for sale

5 Basta con telefonear para reservar un asiento
You need only phone to reserve a seat

6 Basta con un error para que todo se estropee
One single error is enough to ruin everything

7 Aún falta cerrar las maletas
We/One still have/has to close the suitcases

8 Hay una habitación libre
There is one spare room
No había cartas esta mañana
There were no letters this morning

9 Hay que cerrar las puertas
We have/One has to shut the doors

10 Hace calor/viento/sol
It is hot/windy/sunny
Mañana hará bueno
It'll be nice (weather) tomorrow

11 Hace seis meses que vivo/vivimos aquí
I/we have lived *or* been living here for six months

12 Hace tres años que no le veo
It is three years since I last saw him

Impersonal Verbs (contd)

INFINITIVE	CONSTRUCTION
hacer falta	**hace falta** + noun object (+ indirect object) (→1)
	(somebody) needs something, something is necessary (to somebody)
	hace falta + infinitive (+ indirect object) (→2)
	it is necessary to do
	hace falta que + subjunctive (→3)
	it is necessary to do, somebody must do
parecer	**parece que** (+ indirect object) + indicative (→4)
	it seems/appears that
ser	**es/son** + time expression (→5)
	it is
	es + **de día/noche** (→6)
	it is
	es + adjective + infinitive (→7)
	it is
ser mejor	**es mejor** + infinitive (→8)
	it's better to do
	es mejor que + subjunctive (→9)
	it's better if/that
valer más	**más vale** + infinitive (→10)
	it's better to do
	más vale que + subjunctive (→11)
	it's better to do/that somebody does

1 Hace falta valor para hacer eso
One needs courage to do that; Courage is needed to do that
Me hace falta otro vaso más
I need an extra glass

2 Hace falta volver
It is necessary to return; We/I/You must return*
Me hacía falta volver
I had to return

3 Hace falta que Vd se vaya
You have to/must leave

4 (Me) parece que estás equivocado
It seems (to me) you are wrong

5 Son las tres y media
It is half past three
Ya es primavera
It is Spring now

6 Era de noche cuando llegamos
It was night when we arrived

7 Era inútil protestar
It was useless to complain

8 Es mejor no decir nada
It's better to keep quiet

9 Es mejor que lo pongas aquí
It's better if/that you put it here

10 Más vale prevenir que curar
Prevention is better than cure

11 Más valdría que no fuéramos
It would be better if we didn't go/We'd better not go

*The translation here obviously depends on context

The Infinitive

The infinitive is the form of the verb found in dictionary entries meaning 'to ...', e.g. **hablar** to speak, **vivir** to live.

The infinitive is used in the following ways:
• After a preposition (→**1**)

• As a verbal noun (→**2**)
 In this use the article may precede the infinitive, especially when the infinitive is the subject and begins the sentence (→**3**)

• As a dependent infinitive, in the following verbal constructions:
 —with no linking preposition (→**4**)
 —with the linking preposition **a** (→**5**)
  (see also p 66)
 —with the linking preposition **de** (→**6**)
  (see also p 66)
 —with the linking preposition **en** (→**7**)
  (see also p 66)
 —with the linking preposition **con** (→**8**)
  (see also p 66)
 —with the linking preposition **por** (→**9**)
  (see also p 66)

• The following construction should also be noted:
  indefinite pronoun + **que** + infinitive (→**10**)

• The object pronouns generally follow the infinitive and are attached to it. For exceptions see p 228.

Continued

1 Después de acabar el desayuno, salió de casa
After finishing her breakfast she went out
Al enterarse de lo ocurrido se puso furiosa
When she found out what had happened she was furious
Me hizo daño sin saberlo
She hurt me without her knowing

2 Su deporte preferido es montar a caballo
Her favourite sport is horse riding
Ver es creer
Seeing is believing

3 El viajar tanto me resulta cansado
I find so much travelling tiring

4 ¿Quiere Vd esperar?
Would you like to wait?

5 Aprenderán pronto a nadar
They will soon learn to swim

6 Pronto dejará de llover
It'll stop raining soon

7 La comida tarda en hacerse
The meal is taking a long time to cook

8 Amenazó con denunciarles
He threatened to report them (to the police)

9 Comience Vd por decirme su nombre
Please start by giving me your name

10 Tengo algo que decirte
I have something to tell you

The Infinitive (contd)

The verbs set out below are followed by the infinitive with no linking preposition.

- **deber, poder, saber, querer** and **tener que** (**hay que** in impersonal constructions) (→**1**)

- **valer más, hacer falta:** see Impersonal Verbs, p 44

- verbs of seeing or hearing e.g. **ver** to see, **oír** to hear (→**2**)

- **hacer** (→**3**)

- **dejar** to let, allow (→**3**)

- The following common verbs:

aconsejar	to advise	(→**4**)
conseguir	to manage to	(→**5**)
decidir	to decide	
desear	to wish, want	(→**6**)
esperar	to hope	(→**7**)
evitar	to avoid	(→**8**)
impedir	to prevent	(→**9**)
intentar	to try	(→**10**)
lograr	to manage to	(→**5**)
necesitar	to need	(→**11**)
odiar	to hate	
olvidar	to forget	(→**12**)
pensar	to think	(→**13**)
preferir	to prefer	(→**14**)
procurar	to try	(→**10**)
prohibir	to forbid	(→**15**)
prometer	to promise	(→**16**)
proponer	to propose	(→**17**)

Continued

1 **¿Quiere Vd esperar?**
Would you like to wait?
No puede venir
She can't come

2 **Nos ha visto llegar**   **Se les oye cantar**
She saw us arriving   You can hear them singing

3 **No me hagas reír**   **Déjeme pasar**
Don't make me laugh   Let me past

4 **Le aconsejamos dejarlo para mañana**
We advise you to leave it until tomorrow

5 **Aún no he conseguido/logrado entenderlo**
I still haven't managed to understand it

6 **No desea tener más hijos**
She doesn't want to have any more children

7 **Esperamos ir de vacaciones este verano**
We are hoping to go on holiday this summer

8 **Evite beber cuando conduzca**
Avoid drinking and driving

9 **No pudo impedirle hablar**
He couldn't prevent him from speaking

10 **Intentamos/procuramos pasar desapercibidos**
We tried not to be noticed

11 **Necesitaba salir a la calle**
I/he/she needed to go out

12 **Olvidó dejar su dirección**
He/she forgot to leave his/her address

13 **¿Piensan venir por Navidad?**
Are you thinking of coming for Christmas?

14 **Preferiría elegirlo yo mismo**
I'd rather choose it myself

15 **Prohibió fumar a los alumnos**
He forbade the pupils to smoke

16 **Prometieron volver pronto**
They promised to come back soon

17 **Propongo salir cuanto antes**
I propose to leave as soon as possible

50   VERBS

The Infinitive: Set Expressions

The following are set in Spanish with the meaning shown:

dejar caer	to drop	(→1)
hacer entrar	to show in	(→2)
hacer saber	to let know, make known	(→3)
hacer salir	to let out	(→4)
hacer venir	to send for	(→5)
ir(se) a buscar	to go for, go and get	(→6)
mandar hacer	to order	(→7)
mandar llamar	to send for	(→8)
oír decir que	to hear it said that	(→9)
oír hablar de	to hear of/about	(→10)
querer decir	to mean	(→11)

The Perfect Infinitive

• The perfect infinitive is formed using the auxiliary verb **haber** with the past participle of the verb (→12)

• The perfect infinitive is found:
  – following certain prepositions, especially **después de** *after* (→13)
  – following certain verbal constructions (→14)

1 Al verlo, dejó caer lo que llevaba en las manos
When he saw him he dropped what he was carrying

2 Haz entrar a nuestros invitados
Show our guests in

3 Quiero hacerles saber que no serán bien recibidos
I want to let them know that they won't be welcome

4 Hágale salir, por favor
Please let him out

5 Le he hecho venir a Vd porque ...
I sent for you because ...

6 Vete a buscar los guantes
Go and get your gloves

7 Me he mandado hacer un traje
I have ordered a suit

8 Mandaron llamar al médico
They sent for the doctor

9 He oído decir que está enfermo
I've heard it said that he's ill

10 No he oído hablar más de él
I haven't heard anything more (said) of him

11 ¿Qué quiere decir eso?
What does that mean?

12 haber terminado   **haberse vestido**
to have finished   to have got dressed

13 Después de haber comprado el regalo, volvió a casa
After buying/having bought the present, he went back home
Después de haber madrugado tanto, el taxi se retrasó
After she got up so early, the taxi arrived late

14 perdonar a alguien por haber hecho
to forgive somebody for doing/having done
dar las gracias a alguien por haber hecho
to thank somebody for doing/having done
pedir perdón por haber hecho
to be sorry for doing/having done

The Gerund

Formation

- 1st conjugation
  Replace the **-ar** of the infinitive by **-ando** (→**1**)
- 2nd conjugation
  Replace the **-er** of the infinitive by **-iendo** (→**2**)
- 3rd conjugation
  Replace the **-ir** of the infinitive by **-iendo** (→**3**)
- For irregular gerunds, see irregular verbs, p 80 ff.

Uses

- After the verb **estar**, to form the continuous tenses (→**4**)
- After the verbs **seguir** and **continuar** *to continue*, and **ir** when meaning *to happen gradually* (→**5**)
- In time constructions, after **llevar** (→**6**)
- When the action in the main clause needs to be complemented by another action (→**7**)
- The position of object pronouns is the same as for the infinitive (see p 46)
- The gerund is invariable and strictly verbal in sense.

The Present Participle

- It is formed by replacing the **-ar** of the infinitive of 1st conjugation verbs by **-ante**, and the **-er** and **-ir** of the 2nd and 3rd conjugations by **-iente** (→**8**)
- A very limited number of verbs have a present participle, which is either used as an adjective or a noun (→**9/10**)

1 cantar → **cantando**
  to sing   singing
2 temer → **temiendo**
  to fear   fearing
3 partir → **partiendo**
  to leave   leaving
4 Estoy escribiendo una carta
  I am writing a letter
  Estaban esperándonos
  They were waiting for us
5 Sigue viniendo todos los días
  He/she is still coming every day
  Continuarán subiendo los precios
  Prices will continue to go up
  El ejército iba avanzando poco a poco
  The army was gradually advancing
6 Lleva dos años estudiando inglés
  He/she has been studying English for two years
7 Pasamos el día tomando el sol en la playa
  We spent the day sunbathing on the beach
  Iba cojeando
  He/she/I was limping
  Salieron corriendo
  They ran out
8 cantar → **cantante**
  to sing   singing/singer
  pender → **pendiente**
  to hang   hanging
  seguir → **siguiente**
  to follow   following
9 agua corriente
  running water
10 un estudiante
  a student

Use of Tenses

The Present

- Unlike English, Spanish often uses the same verb form for the simple present (e.g. *I smoke, he reads, we live*) and the continuous present (e.g. *I am smoking, he is reading, we are living*) (→**1**)
- Normally, however, the continuous present is used to translate the English:
  to be doing   **estar haciendo** (→**2**)
- Spanish uses the present tense where English uses the perfect in the following cases:
  - with certain prepositions of time – notably **desde** *for/since* – when an action begun in the past is continued in the present (→**3**)
    Note, however, that the perfect can be used as in English when the verb is negative (→**4**)
  - in the construction **acabar de hacer** *to have just done* (→**5**)
- Like English, Spanish often uses the present where a future action is implied (→**6**)

The Future

The future is generally used as in English (→**7**), but note the following:
- Immediate future time is often expressed by means of the present tense of **ir** + **a** + infinitive (→**8**)
- When *'will'* or *'shall'* mean *'wish to'*, *'are willing to'*, **querer** is used (→**9**)

The Future Perfect

- Used as in English *shall/will have done* (→**10**)
- It can also express conjecture, usually about things in the recent past (→**11**)

Continued

1 **Fumo** I smoke *or* I am smoking
  Lee He reads *or* He is reading
  Vivimos We live *or* We are living
2 **Está fumando**
  He is smoking
3 **Linda estudia español desde hace seis meses**
  Linda's been learning Spanish for six months (*and still is*)
  Estoy de pie desde las siete
  I've been up since seven
  ¿Hace mucho que esperan?
  Have you been waiting long?
  Ya hace dos semanas que estamos aquí
  That's two weeks we've been here (now)
4 **No se han visto desde hace meses**
  They haven't seen each other for months
5 **Isabel acaba de salir**
  Isabel has just left
6 **Mañana voy a Madrid**
  I am going to Madrid tomorrow
7 **Lo haré mañana**
  I'll do it tomorrow
8 **Te vas a caer si no tienes cuidado**
  You'll fall if you're not careful
  Va a perder el tren
  He's going to miss the train
  Va a llevar una media hora
  It'll take about half an hour
9 **¿Me quieres esperar un momento, por favor?**
  Will you wait for me a second, please?
10 **Lo habré acabado para mañana**
   I will have finished it for tomorrow
11 **Ya habrán llegado a casa**
   They must have arrived home by now

Use of Tenses (contd)

The Imperfect

- The imperfect describes:
  - an action or state in the past without definite limits in time (→**1**)
  - habitual action(s) in the past (often expressed in English by means of *would* or *used to*) (→**2**)
- Spanish uses the imperfect tense where English uses the pluperfect in the following cases:
  - with certain prepositions of time – notably **desde** *for/since* – when an action begun in the remoter past was continued in the more recent past (→**3**)
    Note, however, that the pluperfect is used as in English when the verb is negative or the action has been completed (→**4**)
  - in the construction **acabar de hacer** *to have just done* (→**5**)
- Both the continuous and simple forms in English can be translated by the Spanish simple imperfect, but the continuous imperfect is used when the emphasis is on the fact that an action was going on at a precise moment in the past (→**6**)

The Perfect

- The perfect is generally used as in English (→**7**)

The Preterite

- The preterite generally corresponds to the English simple past in both written and spoken Spanish (→**8**)
  However, while English can use the simple past to describe habitual actions or settings, Spanish uses the imperfect (see above) (→**9**)

The Past Anterior

- This tense is only ever used in written, literary Spanish, to replace the pluperfect in time clauses where the verb in the main clause is in the preterite (→**10**)

1 Todos mirábamos en silencio
We were all watching in silence
Nuestras habitaciones daban a la playa
Our rooms overlooked the beach
2 En su juventud se levantaba de madrugada
In his youth he got up at dawn
Hablábamos sin parar durante horas
We would talk non-stop for hours on end
Mi hermano siempre me tomaba el pelo
My brother always used to tease me
3 Hacía dos años que vivíamos en Irlanda
We had been living in Ireland for two years
Estaba enfermo desde 1990
He had been ill since 1990
Hacía mucho tiempo que salían juntos
They had been going out together for a long time
4 Hacía un año que no le había visto
I hadn't seen him for a year
Hacía una hora que había llegado
She had arrived an hour before
5 Acababa de encontrármelos
I had just met them
6 Cuando llegué, todos estaban fumando
When I arrived, they were all smoking
7 Todavía no han salido
They haven't come out yet
8 Me desperté y salté de la cama
I woke up and jumped out of bed
9 Siempre iban en coche al trabajo
They always travelled to work by car
10 Apenas hubo acabado, se oyeron unos golpes en la puerta
She had scarcely finished when there was a knock at the door

The Subjunctive: when to use it

(For how to form the subjunctive see pp 6 ff.)

- After verbs of:
  - 'wishing'
    querer que
    desear que } to wish that, want (→1)
  - 'emotion' (e.g. regret, surprise, shame, pleasure, etc)
    sentir que   to be sorry that (→2)
    sorprender que   to be surprised that (→3)
    alegrarse de que   to be pleased that (→4)
  - 'asking' and 'advising'
    pedir que   to ask that (→5)
    aconsejar que   to advise that (→6)

In all the above constructions, when the subject of the verbs in the main and subordinate clause is the same, the infinitive is used, and the conjunction **que** omitted (→7)

  - 'ordering', 'forbidding',
    'allowing'
    mandar que*
    ordenar que* } to order that (→8)
    permitir que*
    dejar que*   } to allow that (→9)
    prohibir que*   to forbid that (→10)
    impedir que*   to prevent that (→11)

*With these verbs either the subjunctive or the infinitive is used when the object of the main verb is the subject of the subordinate verb (→12)

- Always after verbs expressing doubt or uncertainty, and verbs of opinion used negatively
    dudar que   to doubt that (→13)
    no creer que
    no pensar que } not to think that (→14)

Continued

1 **Queremos que esté contenta**
   We want her to be happy (literally: We want that she is happy)
   ¿Desea Vd que lo haga yo?
   Do you want me to do it?
2 **Sentí mucho que no vinieran**
   I was very sorry that they didn't come
3 **Nos sorprendió que no les vieran Vds**
   We were surprised you didn't see them
4 **Me alegro de que te gusten**
   I'm pleased that you like them
5 **Solo les pedimos que tengan cuidado**
   We're only asking you to take care
6 **Le aconsejé que no llegara tarde**
   I advised him not to be late
7 **Quiero que lo termines pronto**
   I want you to finish it soon
   but
   Quiero terminarlo pronto
   I want to finish it soon
8 **Ha mandado que vuelvan**
   He has ordered them to come back
   Ordenó que fueran castigados
   He ordered them to be punished
9 **No permitas que te tomen el pelo**
   Don't let them pull your leg
   No me dejó que la llevara a casa
   She didn't allow me to take her home
10 **Te prohíbo que digas eso**
   I forbid you to say that
11 **No les impido que vengan**
   I am not preventing them from coming
12 **Les ordenó que salieran** *or* **Les ordenó salir**
   She ordered them to go out
13 **Dudo que lo sepan hacer**
   I doubt they can do it
14 **No creo que sean tan listos**
   I don't think they are as clever as that

The Subjunctive: when to use it (contd)

● In impersonal constructions which express necessity, possibility, etc

hace falta que
es necesario que   } *it is necessary that* (→1)

es posible que   *it is possible that* (→2)

más vale que   *it is better that* (→3)

es una lástima que   *it is a pity that* (→4)

Note that in impersonal constructions which state a fact or express certainty the indicative is used when the impersonal verb is affirmative. When it is negative, the subjunctive is used (→5)

● After certain conjunctions

para que
a fin de que*   } *so that* (→6)

como si   *as if* (→7)

sin que*   *without* (→8)

a condición de que*
con tal (de) que*   } *provided that,*
siempre que   *on condition that* (→9)

a menos que
a no ser que   } *unless* (→10)

antes (de) que*   *before* (→11)

no sea que   *lest/in case* (→12)

mientras (que)
siempre que   } *as long as* (→13)

(el) que   *the fact that* (→14)

*When the subject of both verbs is the same, the infinitive is used, and the final **que** is omitted (→8)

Continued

1 ¿Hace falta que vaya Jaime?
Does James have to go?

2 Es posible que tengan razón
It's possible that they are right

3 Más vale que se quede Vd en su casa
It's better that you stay at home

4 Es una lástima que haya perdido su perrito
It's a shame/pity that she has lost her puppy

5 Es verdad que va a venir
It's true that he's coming
but
No es verdad que vayan a hacerlo
It's not true that they are going to do it

6 Átalas bien para que no se caigan
Tie them up tightly so that they won't fall

7 Hablaba como si no creyera en sus propias palabras
He talked as if he didn't believe in his own words

8 Salimos sin que nos vieran
We left without them seeing us
but
Me fui sin esperarla
I went without waiting for her

9 Lo haré con tal de que me cuentes todo lo que pasó
I'll do it provided you tell me all that happened

10 Saldremos de paseo a menos que esté lloviendo
We'll go for a walk unless it's raining

11 Avísale antes de que sea demasiado tarde
Warn him before it's too late

12 Habla en voz baja, no sea que alguien nos oiga
Speak softly in case anyone hears us

13 Eso no pasará mientras yo sea el jefe aquí
That won't happen as long as I am the boss here

14 El que no me escribiera no me importaba demasiado
The fact that he didn't write didn't matter to me too much

The Subjunctive: when to use it (contd)

• After the conjunctions

> **de modo que**
> **de forma que**
> **de manera que**

so that (indicating a purpose) (→**1**)

Note that when these conjunctions introduce a result and not a purpose the subjunctive is not used (→**2**)

• In relative clauses with an antecedent which is:
  - negative (→**3**)
  - indefinite (→**4**)
  - non-specific (→**5**)

• In main clauses, to express a wish or exhortation. The verb may be preceded by expressions like **ojalá** or **que** (→**6**)

• In the **si** clause of conditions where the English sentence contains a conditional tense (→**7**)

• In set expressions (→**8**)

• In the following constructions which translate *however*:
  - **por** + adjective + subjunctive (→**9**)
  - **por** + adverb + subjunctive (→**10**)
  - **por** + **mucho** + subjunctive (→**11**)

Continued

1 **Vuélvanse de manera que les vea bien**
   Turn round so that I can see you properly
2 **No quieren hacerlo, de manera que tendré que hacerlo yo**
   They won't do it, so I'll have to do it myself
3 **No he encontrado a nadie que la conociera**
   I haven't met anyone who knows her
   No dijo nada que no supiéramos ya
   He/she didn't say anything we didn't already know
4 **Necesito alguien que sepa conducir**
   I need someone who can drive
   Busco algo que me distraiga
   I'm looking for something to take my mind off it
5 **Busca una casa que tenga calefacción central**
   He/she's looking for a house which has central heating
   (*subjunctive used since such a house may or may not exist*)
   El que lo haya visto tiene que decírmelo
   Anyone who has seen it must tell me
   (*subjunctive used since it is not known who has seen it*)
6 **¡Ojalá haga buen tiempo!**
   Let's hope the weather will be good!
   ¡Que te diviertas!
   Have a good time!
7 **Si fuéramos en coche llegaríamos a tiempo**
   If we went by car we'd be there in time
8 **Diga lo que diga ...**   **Sea lo que sea ...**
   Whatever he may say ...   Be that as it may ...
   Pase lo que pase ...   **Sea como sea ...**
   Come what may ...   One way or another ...
9 **Por cansado que esté, seguirá trabajando**
   No matter how/however tired he may be, he'll go on working
10 **Por lejos que viva, iremos a buscarle**
   No matter how/however far away he lives, we'll go and look
   for him
11 **Por mucho que lo intente, nunca lo conseguirá**
   No matter how/however hard he tries, he'll never succeed

The Subjunctive (contd)

Clauses taking either a subjunctive or an indicative

In certain constructions, a subjunctive is needed when the action refers to future events or hypothetical situations, whereas an indicative is used when stating a fact or experience (→1)

The commonest of these are:

- The conjunctions

cuando	*when* (→1)
en cuanto }	*as soon as* (→2)
tan pronto como	
después (de) que*	*after* (→3)
hasta que	*until* (→4)
mientras	*while* (→5)
siempre que	*whenever* (→6)
aunque	*even though* (→7)

all conjunctions and pronouns ending in **-quiera** (*-ever*) (→8)

*Note that if the subject of both verbs is the same, the subjunctive introduced by **después (de) que** may be replaced by **después de** + infinitive (→9)

Sequence of tenses in Subordinate Clauses

- If the verb in the main clause is in the present, future or imperative, the verb in the dependent clause will be in the present or perfect subjunctive (→10)

- If the verb in the main clause is in the conditional or any past tense, the verb in the dependent clause will be in the imperfect or pluperfect subjunctive (→11)

1 Le aconsejé que oyera música cuando estuviera nervioso
I advised him to listen to music when he felt nervous
Me gusta nadar cuando hace calor
I like to swim when it is warm

2 Te devolveré el libro tan pronto como lo haya leído
I'll give you back the book as soon as I have read it

3 Te lo diré después de que te hayas sentado
I'll tell you after you've sat down

4 Quédate aquí hasta que volvamos
Stay here until we come back

5 No hablen en voz alta mientras estén ellos aquí
Don't speak loudly while they are here

6 Vuelvan por aquí siempre que quieran
Come back whenever you wish to

7 No le creeré aunque diga la verdad
I won't believe him even if he tells the truth

8 La encontraré dondequiera que esté
I will find her wherever she might be

9 Después de cenar nos fuimos al cine
After dinner we went to the cinema

10 Quiero que lo hagas (pres + pres subj)
I want you to do it
Temo que no haya venido (pres + perf subj)
I fear he hasn't come (might not have come)
Iremos por aquí para que no nos vean (future + pres subj)
We'll go this way so that they won't see us

11 Me gustaría que llegaras temprano (cond + imperf subj)
I'd like you to arrive early
Les pedí que me esperaran (preterite + imperf subj)
I asked them to wait for me
Sentiría mucho que hubiese muerto (cond + pluperf subj)
I would be very sorry if he were dead

Verbs governing a, de, con, en, por and para

The following lists (pp 66 to 73) contain common verbal constructions using the prepositions **a**, **de**, **con**, **en**, **por** and **para**.

Note the following abbreviations:

infin	infinitive
perf infin	perfect infinitive*
algn	alguien
sb	somebody
sth	something

*For formation see p 50

aburrirse de + infin	*to get bored with doing* (→**1**)
acabar con algo/algn	*to put an end to sth/finish with sb* (→**2**)
acabar de* + infin	*to have just done* (→**3**)
acabar por + infin	*to end up doing* (→**4**)
acercarse a algo/algn	*to approach sth/sb*
acordarse de algo/algn/de + infin	*to remember sth/sb/doing* (→**5**)
acostumbrarse a algo/algn/a + infin	*to get used to sth/sb/to doing* (→**6**)
acusar a algn de algo/de + perf infin	*to accuse sb of sth/of doing, having done* (→**7**)
advertir a algn de algo	*to notify, warn sb about sth* (→**8**)
aficionarse a algo/a + infin	*to grow fond of sth/of doing* (→**9**)
alegrarse de algo/de + perf infin	*to be glad about sth/of doing, having done* (→**10**)
alejarse de algn/algo	*to move away from sb/sth*
amenazar a algn con algo/con + infin	*to threaten sb with sth/to do* (→**11**)
animar a algn a + infin	*to encourage sb to do*
apresurarse a + infin	*to hurry to do* (→**12**)

*See also Use of Tenses, pp 54 and 56

Continued

1 Me aburría de no poder salir de casa
I used to get bored with not being able to leave the house

2 Quiso acabar con su vida
He wanted to put an end to his life

3 Acababan de llegar cuando ...
They had just arrived when ...

4 El acusado acabó por confesarlo todo
The accused ended up by confessing everything

5 Nos acordamos muy bien de aquellas vacaciones
We remember that holiday very well

6 Me he acostumbrado a levantarme temprano
I've got used to getting up early

7 Le acusó de haber mentido
She accused him of lying

8 Advertí a mi amigo del peligro que corría
I warned my friend about the danger he was in

9 Nos hemos aficionado a la música clásica
We've grown fond of classical music

10 Me alegro de haberle conocido
I'm glad I met him

11 Amenazó con denunciarles
He threatened to report them

12 Se apresuraron a coger sitio
They hurried to find a seat

Verbs governing a, de, con, en, por and para (contd)

aprender a + infin	to learn to do (→1)
aprovecharse de algo/algn	to take advantage of sth/sb
aproximarse a algn/algo	to approach sb/sth
asistir a algo	to attend sth, be at sth
asomarse a/por	to lean out of (→2)
asombrarse de + infin	to be surprised at doing (→3)
atreverse a + infin	to dare to do
avergonzarse de algo/algn/de + perf infin	to be ashamed of sth/sb/of doing, having done (→4)
ayudar a algn a + infin	to help sb to do (→5)
bajarse de (+ place/vehicle)	to get off/out of (→6)
burlarse de algn	to make fun of sb
cansarse de algo/algn/de + infin	to tire of sth/sb/of doing
carecer de algo	to lack sth (→7)
cargar de algo	to load with sth (→8)
casarse con algn	to get married to sb (→9)
cesar de + infin	to stop doing
chocar con algo	to crash/bump into sth (→10)
comenzar a + infin	to begin to do
comparar con algn/algo	to compare with sb/sth
consentir en + infin	to agree to do
consistir en + infin	to consist of doing (→11)
constar de algo	to consist of sth (→12)
contar con algn/algo	to rely on sb/sth (→13)
convenir en + infin	to agree to do (→14)
darse cuenta de algo	to realise sth
dejar de + infin	to stop doing (→15)
depender de algo/algn	to depend on sth/sb (→16)
despedirse de algn	to say goodbye to sb
dirigirse a + place/a algn	to head for/address sb
disponerse a + infin	to get ready to do
empezar a + infin	to begin to do
empezar por + infin	to begin by doing (→17)

Continued

1 **Me gustaría aprender a nadar**
I'd like to learn to swim

2 **No te asomes a la ventana**
Don't lean out of the window

3 **Nos asombramos mucho de verles ahí**
We were very surprised at seeing them there

4 **No me avergüenzo de haberlo hecho**
I'm not ashamed of having done it

5 **Ayúdeme a llevar estas maletas**
Help me to carry these cases

6 **Se bajó del coche**
He got out of the car

7 **La casa carecía de jardín**
The house lacked (did not have) a garden

8 **El carro iba cargado de paja**
The cart was loaded with straw

9 **Se casó con Andrés**
She married Andrew

10 **Enciende la luz, o chocarás con la puerta**
Turn the light on, or you'll bump into the door

11 **Mi plan consistía en vigilarles de cerca**
My plan consisted of keeping a close eye on them

12 **El examen consta de tres partes**
The exam consists of three parts

13 **Cuento contigo para que me ayudes a hacerlo**
I rely on you to help me do it

14 **Convinieron en reunirse al día siguiente**
They agreed to meet the following day

15 **¿Quieres dejar de hablar?**
Will you stop talking?

16 **No depende de mí**
It doesn't depend on me

17 **Empieza por enterarte de lo que se trata**
Begin by finding out what it is about

Verbs governing a, de, con, en, por and para (contd)

encontrarse con algn	to meet sb (by chance) (→**1**)
enfadarse con algn	to get annoyed with sb
enseñar a algn a + infin	to teach sb to (→**2**)
enterarse de algo	to find out about sth (→**3**)
entrar en (+ place)	to enter, go into
esperar a + infin	to wait until (→**4**)
estar de acuerdo con algn/ algo	to agree with sb/sth
fiarse de algn/algo	to trust sb/sth
fijarse en algo/algn	to notice sth/sb (→**5**)
hablar con algn	to talk to sb (→**6**)
hacer caso a algn	to pay attention to sb
hartarse de algo/algn/de + infin	to get fed up with sth/sb/with doing (→**7**)
interesarse por algo/algn	to be interested in sth/sb (→**8**)
invitar a algn a + infin	to invite sb to do
jugar a (+ sports, games)	to play
llegar a (+ place)/a + infin	to reach/to manage to do (→**9**)
llenar de algo	to fill with sth
luchar por algo/por + infin	to fight, strive for/to do (→**10**)
negarse a + infin	to refuse to do (→**11**)
obligar a algn a + infin	to make sb do (→**12**)
ocuparse de algn/algo	to take care of sb/attend to sth
oler a algo	to smell of sth (→**13**)
olvidarse de algo/algn/de + infin	to forget sth/sb/to do (→**14**)
oponerse a algo/a + infin	to be opposed to sth/to doing
parecerse a algn/algo	to resemble sb/sth
pensar en algo/algn/en + infin	to think about sth/sb/about doing (→**15**)
preguntar por algn	to ask for/about sb
preocuparse de or por algo/ algn	to worry about sth/sb (→**16**)

Continued

1 Me encontré con ella al entrar en el Banco
I met her as I was entering the Bank

2 Le estoy enseñando a nadar
I am teaching him to swim

3 ¿Te has enterado del sitio adonde hay que ir?
Have you found out where we have to go?

4 Espera a saber lo que quiere antes de comprar el regalo
Wait until you know what he wants before buying the present

5 Me fijé en él cuando subía a su coche
I noticed him when he was getting into his car

6 ¿Puedo hablar con Vd un momento?
May I talk to you for a moment?

7 Me he hartado de escribirle
I've got fed up with writing to him

8 Me interesaba mucho por la arqueología
I was very interested in archaeology

9 Lo intenté sin llegar a conseguirlo
I tried without managing to do it

10 Hay que luchar por mantener la paz
One must strive to preserve peace

11 Se negó a hacerlo
He refused to do it

12 Le obligó a sentarse
He made him sit down

13 Este perfume huele a jazmín
This perfume smells of jasmine

14 Siempre me olvido de cerrar la puerta
I always forget to shut the door

15 No quiero pensar en eso
I don't want to think about that

16 Se preocupa mucho de/por su apariencia
He worries a lot about his appearance

Verbs governing a, de, con, en, por and para (contd)

prepararse a + infin	to prepare to do
probar a + infin	to try to do
quedar en + infin	to agree to do (→1)
quedar por + infin	to remain to be done (→2)
quejarse de algo	to complain of sth
referirse a algo	to refer to sth
reírse de algo/algn	to laugh at sth/sb
rodear de	to surround with (→3)
romper a + infin	to (suddenly) start to do (→4)
salir de (+ place)	to leave
sentarse a (+ table etc)	to sit down at
subir(se) a (+ vehicle/place)	to get on, into/to climb (→5)
servir de algo a algn	to be useful to/serve sb as sth (→6)
servir para algo/para + infin	to be good as sth/for doing (→7)
servirse de algo	to use sth (→8)
soñar con algn/algo/con + infin	to dream about/of sb/sth/of doing
sorprenderse de algo	to be surprised at sth
tardar en + infin	to take time to do (→9)
tener ganas de algo/de + infin	to want sth/to do (→10)
tener miedo de algo	to be afraid of sth (→11)
tener miedo a algn	to be afraid of sb (→12)
terminar por + infin	to end by doing
tirar de algo/algn	to pull sth/sb
trabajar de (+ occupation)	to work as (→13)
trabajar en (+ place of work)	to work at/in (→14)
traducir a (+ language)	to translate into
tratar de + infin	to try to do (→15)
tratarse de algo/algn/de + infin	to be a question of sth/about sb/about doing (→16)
vacilar en + infin	to hesitate to do (→17)
volver a + infin	to do again (→18)

1 Habíamos quedado en encontrarnos a las 8
We had agreed to meet at 8

2 Queda por averiguar dónde se ocultan
It remains to be discovered where they are hiding

3 Habían rodeado el jardín de un seto de cipreses
They had surrounded the garden with a hedge of cypress trees

4 Al apagarse la luz, el niño rompió a llorar
When the lights went out, the little boy suddenly started to cry

5 ¡De prisa, sube al coche!
Get into the car, quick!

6 Esto me servirá de bastón
This will serve me as a walking stick

7 No sirvo para (ser) jardinero
I'm no good as a gardener

8 Se sirvió de un destornillador para abrirlo
She used a screwdriver to open it

9 Tardaron mucho en salir
They took a long time to come out

10 Tengo ganas de volver a España
I want to go back to Spain

11 Mi hija tiene miedo de la oscuridad
My daughter is afraid of the dark

12 Nunca tuvieron miedo a su padre
They were never afraid of their father

13 Pedro trabaja de camarero en Londres
Peter works as a waiter in London

14 Trabajaba en una oficina
I used to work in an office

15 No trates de engañarme
Don't try to fool me

16 Se trata de nuestro nuevo vecino
It's about our new neighbour

17 Nunca vacilaban en pedir dinero
They never hesitated to borrow money

18 No vuelvas a hacerlo nunca más
Don't ever do it again

Ser and Estar

Spanish has two verbs — **ser** and **estar** — for *to be*.
They are not interchangeable and each one is used in defined contexts.

ser is used:

• With an adjective, to express a permanent or inherent quality (→**1**)
• To express occupation or nationality (→**2**)
• To express possession (→**3**)
• To express origin or the material from which something is made (→**4**)
• With a noun, pronoun or infinitive following the verb (→**5**)
• To express the time and date (→**6**)
• To form the passive, with the past participle (see p 32).
  Note that this use emphasizes the action of the verb. If, however, the resultant state or condition needs to be emphasized, **estar** is used. The past participle then functions as an adjective (see p 204) and has to agree in gender and in number with the noun (→**7**)

estar is used:

• Always, to indicate place or location (→**8**)
• With an adjective or adjectival phrase, to express a quality or state seen by the speaker as subject to change or different from expected (→**9**)
• When speaking of a person's state of health (→**10**)
• To form the continuous tenses, used with the gerund (see p 52) (→**11**)
• With **de** + noun, to indicate a temporary occupation (→**12**)

Continued

1 **Mi hermano es alto**   **María es inteligente**
  My brother is tall   Mary is intelligent
2 **Javier es aviador**   **Sus padres son italianos**
  Javier is an airman   His parents are Italian
3 **La casa es de Miguel**
  The house belongs to Michael
4 **Mi hermana es de Granada**   **Las paredes son de ladrillo**
  My sister is from Granada   The walls are made of brick
5 **Andrés es un niño travieso**
  Andrew is a naughty boy
  Soy yo, Enrique
  It's me, Henry
  Todo es proponérselo
  It's all a question of putting your mind to it
6 **Son las tres y media**   **Mañana es sábado**
  It's half past three   Tomorrow is Saturday
7 **Las puertas eran cerradas sigilosamente**
  The doors were being silently closed
  Las puertas estaban cerradas
  The doors were closed
  (*resultant action*)
8 **La comida está en la mesa**
  The meal is on the table
9 **Su amigo está enfermo**   **El lavabo está ocupado**
  Her friend is ill   The toilet is engaged
  Hoy estoy de mal humor   **Las tiendas están cerradas**
  I'm in a bad mood today   The shops are closed
10 **¿Cómo están Vds?**   **Estamos todos bien**
   How are you?   We are all well
11 **Estamos aprendiendo mucho**
   We are learning a great deal
12 **Mi primo está de médico en un pueblo**
   My cousin works as a doctor in a village

Ser and Estar (contd)

With certain adjectives, both **ser** and **estar** can be used, although they are not interchangeable when used in this way:
- **ser** will express a permanent or inherent quality (→**1**)
- **estar** will express a temporary state or quality (→**2**)

Both **ser** and **estar** may also be used in set expressions.

The commonest of these are:
- With **ser**

Sea como sea	Be that as it may
Es igual/Es lo mismo	It's all the same
llegar a ser	to become
¿Cómo fue eso?	How did that happen?
¿Qué ha sido de él?	What has become of him?
ser para (with the idea of purpose)	to be for (→**3**)

- With **estar**

estar de pie/de rodillas	to be standing/kneeling
estar de viaje	to be travelling
estar de vacaciones	to be on holiday
estar de vuelta	to be back
estar de moda	to be in fashion
Está bien	It's all right
estar para	to be about to do sth/to be in a mood for (→**4**)
estar por	to be inclined to/to be (all) for (→**5**)
estar a punto de	to be just about to do sth (→**6**)

Continued

1 Su hermana es muy joven/vieja
His sister is very young/old
Son muy ricos/pobres
They are very rich/poor
Su amigo era un enfermo
His friend was an invalid
Es un borracho
He is a drunkard
Mi hijo es bueno/malo
My son is good/naughty
Viajar es cansado
Travelling is tiring

2 Está muy joven/vieja con ese vestido
She looks very young/old in that dress
Ahora están muy ricos/pobres
They have become very rich/poor lately
Estaba enfermo
He was ill
Está borracho
He is drunk
Está bueno/malo
He is well/ill
Hoy estoy cansada
I am tired today

3 Este paquete es para Vd
This parcel is for you
Esta caja es para guardar semillas
This box is for keeping seeds in

4 Están para llegar
They're about to arrive

5 Estoy por irme a vivir a España
I'm inclined to go and live in Spain

6 Las rosas están a punto de salir
The roses are about to come out

Verbal Idioms

Special Intransitive Verbs

With the following verbs the Spanish construction is the opposite of the English. The subject in English becomes the indirect object of the Spanish verb, while the object in English becomes the subject of the Spanish verb.

Compare the following:

I like that house (subject: *I*, object: *that house*)

Esa casa me gusta (subject: **esa casa**, indirect object: **me**)

The commonest of these verbs are:

gustar	*to like* (→**1**)
gustar más	*to prefer* (→**2**)
encantar	*(colloquial) to love* (→**3**)
faltar	*to need/to be short of/to have missing* (→**4**)
quedar	*to be/have left* (→**5**)
doler	*to have a pain in/to hurt, ache* (→**6**)
interesar	*to be interested in* (→**7**)
importar	*to mind* (→**8**)

1 Me gusta este vestido
I like this dress (This dress pleases me)

2 Me gustan más éstas
I prefer these

3 Nos encanta hacer deporte
We love sport

4 Me faltaban 100 pesetas
I was short of 100 pesetas
Sólo le falta el toque final
It just needs the finishing touch
Le faltaban tres dientes
He/she had three teeth missing

5 Sólo nos quedan dos kilómetros
We only have two kilometres (left) to go

6 Me duele la cabeza
I have a headache

7 Nos interesa mucho la política
We are very interested in politics

8 No me importa la lluvia
I don't mind the rain

Irregular Verbs

The verbs listed opposite and conjugated on pp 82 to 161 provide the main patterns for irregular verbs. The verbs are grouped opposite according to their infinitive ending and are shown in the following tables in alphabetical order.

In the tables, the most important irregular verbs are given in their most common simple tenses, together with the imperative and the gerund.
The past participle is also shown for each verb, to enable you to form all the compound tenses, as on pp 18 to 23.

The pronouns **ella** and **Vd** take the same verb endings as **él**, while **ellas** and **Vds** take the same endings as **ellos**.

- All the verbs included in the tables differ from the three conjugations set out on pp 8 to 13. Many — e.g. **contar** — serve as models for groups of verbs, while others — e.g. **ir** — are unique. On pp 162 to 186 you will find over 2,800 commonly used verbs listed alphabetically and cross referred either to the relevant basic conjugation or to the appropriate model in the verb tables.

Imperfect Subjunctive of Irregular Verbs

For verbs with an irregular root form in the preterite tense — eg andar → anduvieron — the imperfect subjunctive is formed by using the root form of the 3rd person plural of the preterite tense, and adding the imperfect subjunctive endings -iera/-iese etc where the verb has an 'i' in the preterite ending — eg anduv**ieron** → anduv**iera/iese** —. Where the verb has no 'i' in the preterite ending, add -era/-ese etc — eg produj**eron** → produj**era/ese** —.

'-ar':		'-er':	
	actuar		saber
	almorzar		satisfacer
	andar		ser
	aunar		tener
	avergonzar		torcer
	averiguar		traer
	contar		valer
	cruzar		vencer
	dar		ver
	empezar		volver
	enviar	'-ir':	abolir
	errar		abrir
	estar		adquirir
	jugar		bendecir
	negar		conducir
	pagar		construir
	pensar		cubrir
	rehusar		decir
	rogar		dirigir
	sacar		distinguir
	volcar		dormir
'-er':	caber		elegir
	caer		erguir
	cocer		escribir
	coger		freír
	crecer		gruñir
	entender		ir
	haber		lucir
	hacer		morir
	hay		oír
	leer		pedir
	llover		prohibir
	mover		reír
	nacer		reñir
	oler		reunir
	poder		salir
	poner		seguir
	querer		sentir
	resolver		venir
	romper		zurcir

82 VERBS: IRREGULAR

abolir *to abolish*

PAST PARTICIPLE
abolido

GERUND
aboliendo

IMPERATIVE
abolid

PRESENT *		*PRESENT SUBJUNCTIVE* not used
nosotros	abolimos	
vosotros	abolís	

FUTURE		*CONDITIONAL*	
yo	aboliré	yo	aboliría
tú	abolirás	tú	abolirías
él	abolirá	él	aboliría
nosotros	aboliremos	nosotros	aboliríamos
vosotros	aboliréis	vosotros	aboliríais
ellos	abolirán	ellos	abolirían

IMPERFECT		*PRETERITE*	
yo	abolía	yo	abolí
tú	abolías	tú	aboliste
él	abolía	él	abolió
nosotros	abolíamos	nosotros	abolimos
vosotros	abolíais	vosotros	abolisteis
ellos	abolían	ellos	abolieron

*present tense only used in persons shown

abrir *to open*

PAST PARTICIPLE
abierto

IMPERATIVE
abre
abri**d**

GERUND
abri**endo**

PRESENT		*PRESENT SUBJUNCTIVE*	
yo	abro	yo	abra
tú	abres	tú	abras
él	abre	él	abra
nosotros	abrimos	nosotros	abramos
vosotros	abrís	vosotros	abráis
ellos	abren	ellos	abran

FUTURE		*CONDITIONAL*	
yo	abriré	yo	abriría
tú	abrirás	tú	abrirías
él	abrirá	él	abriría
nosotros	abriremos	nosotros	abriríamos
vosotros	abriréis	vosotros	abriríais
ellos	abrirán	ellos	abrirían

IMPERFECT		*PRETERITE*	
yo	abría	yo	abrí
tú	abrías	tú	abriste
él	abría	él	abrió
nosotros	abríamos	nosotros	abrimos
vosotros	abríais	vosotros	abristeis
ellos	abrían	ellos	abrieron

actuar *to act*

PAST PARTICIPLE
actuado

IMPERATIVE
actúa
actuad

GERUND
actuando

PRESENT		PRESENT SUBJUNCTIVE	
yo	**actúo**	yo	**actúe**
tú	**actúas**	tú	**actúes**
él	**actúa**	él	**actúe**
nosotros	actuamos	nosotros	actuemos
vosotros	actuáis	vosotros	actuéis
ellos	**actúan**	ellos	**actúen**

FUTURE		CONDITIONAL	
yo	actuaré	yo	actuaría
tú	actuarás	tú	actuarías
él	actuará	él	actuaría
nosotros	actuaremos	nosotros	actuaríamos
vosotros	actuaréis	vosotros	actuaríais
ellos	actuarán	ellos	actuarían

IMPERFECT		PRETERITE	
yo	actuaba	yo	actué
tú	actuabas	tú	actuaste
él	actuaba	él	actuó
nosotros	actuábamos	nosotros	actuamos
vosotros	actuabais	vosotros	actuasteis
ellos	actuaban	ellos	actuaron

adquirir to acquire

PAST PARTICIPLE
adqui**rido**

IMPERATIVE
adquiere
adqui**rid**

GERUND
adquir**iendo**

PRESENT
yo	**adquiero**
tú	**adquieres**
él	**adquiere**
nosotros	adquirimos
vosotros	adquirís
ellos	**adquieren**

PRESENT SUBJUNCTIVE
yo	**adquiera**
tú	**adquieras**
él	**adquiera**
nosotros	**adquramos**
vosotros	adquráis
ellos	**adquieran**

FUTURE
yo	adquiriré
tú	adquirirás
él	adquirirá
nosotros	adquiriremos
vosotros	adquiriréis
ellos	adquirirán

CONDITIONAL
yo	adquiriría
tú	adquirirías
él	adquiriría
nosotros	adquiriríamos
vosotros	adquiriríais
ellos	adquirirían

IMPERFECT
yo	adquiría
tú	adquirías
él	adquiría
nosotros	adquiríamos
vosotros	adquiríais
ellos	adquirían

PRETERITE
yo	adquirí
tú	adquir**iste**
él	adquir**ió**
nosotros	adquirimos
vosotros	adquir**isteis**
ellos	adquir**ieron**

almorzar *to have lunch*

PAST PARTICIPLE
almorzado

IMPERATIVE
almuerza
almorzad

GERUND
almorzando

PRESENT

yo	**almuerzo**
tú	**almuerzas**
él	**almuerza**
nosotros	**almorzamos**
vosotros	**almorzáis**
ellos	**almuerzan**

FUTURE

yo	almorzaré
tú	almorzarás
él	almorzará
nosotros	almorzaremos
vosotros	almorzaréis
ellos	almorzarán

IMPERFECT

yo	almorzaba
tú	almorzabas
él	almorzaba
nosotros	almorzábamos
vosotros	almorzabais
ellos	almorzaban

PRESENT SUBJUNCTIVE

yo	**almuerce**
tú	**almuerces**
él	**almuerce**
nosotros	**almorcemos**
vosotros	**almorcéis**
ellos	**almuercen**

CONDITIONAL

yo	almorzaría
tú	almorzarías
él	almorzaría
nosotros	almorzaríamos
vosotros	almorzaríais
ellos	almorzarían

PRETERITE

yo	**almorcé**
tú	almorzaste
él	almorzó
nosotros	almorzamos
vosotros	almorzasteis
ellos	almorzaron

andar *to walk*

PAST PARTICIPLE andado	*IMPERATIVE* anda andad
GERUND andando	

PRESENT		*PRESENT SUBJUNCTIVE*	
yo	ando	yo	ande
tú	andas	tú	andes
él	anda	él	ande
nosotros	andamos	nosotros	andemos
vosotros	andáis	vosotros	andéis
ellos	andan	ellos	anden

FUTURE		*CONDITIONAL*	
yo	andaré	yo	andaría
tú	andarás	tú	andarías
él	andará	él	andaría
nosotros	andaremos	nosotros	andaríamos
vosotros	andaréis	vosotros	andaríais
ellos	andarán	ellos	andarían

IMPERFECT		*PRETERITE*	
yo	andaba	yo	anduve
tú	andabas	tú	anduviste
él	andaba	él	anduvo
nosotros	andábamos	nosotros	anduvimos
vosotros	andabais	vosotros	anduvisteis
ellos	andaban	ellos	anduvieron

aunar *to join together*

PAST PARTICIPLE
aunado

IMPERATIVE
aúna
aunad

GERUND
aunando

PRESENT

yo	aúno
tú	aúnas
él	aúna
nosotros	aunamos
vosotros	aunáis
ellos	aúnan

FUTURE

yo	aunaré
tú	aunarás
él	aunará
nosotros	aunaremos
vosotros	aunaréis
ellos	aunarán

IMPERFECT

yo	aunaba
tú	aunabas
él	aunaba
nosotros	aunábamos
vosotros	aunabais
ellos	aunaban

PRESENT SUBJUNCTIVE

yo	aúne
tú	aúnes
él	aúne
nosotros	aunemos
vosotros	aunéis
ellos	aúnen

CONDITIONAL

yo	aunaría
tú	aunarías
él	aunaría
nosotros	aunaríamos
vosotros	aunaríais
ellos	aunarían

PRETERITE

yo	auné
tú	aunaste
él	aunó
nosotros	aunamos
vosotros	aunasteis
ellos	aunaron

avergonzar *to shame*

PAST PARTICIPLE
avergonz**ado**

IMPERATIVE
avergüenza
avergonz**ad**

GERUND
avergonz**ando**

PRESENT

yo	avergüenzo
tú	avergüenzas
él	avergüenza
nosotros	avergonzamos
vosotros	avergonzáis
ellos	avergüenzan

PRESENT SUBJUNCTIVE

yo	avergüence
tú	avergüences
él	avergüence
nosotros	avergoncemos
vosotros	avergoncéis
ellos	avergüencen

FUTURE

yo	avergonzaré
tú	avergonzarás
él	avergonzará
nosotros	avergonzaremos
vosotros	avergonzaréis
ellos	avergonzarán

CONDITIONAL

yo	avergonzaría
tú	avergonzarías
él	avergonzaría
nosotros	avergonzaríamos
vosotros	avergonzaríais
ellos	avergonzarían

IMPERFECT

yo	avergonzaba
tú	avergonzabas
él	avergonzaba
nosotros	avergonzábamos
vosotros	avergonzabais
ellos	avergonzaban

PRETERITE

yo	avergoncé
tú	avergonzaste
él	avergonzó
nosotros	avergonzamos
vosotros	avergonzasteis
ellos	avergonzaron

averiguar to find out

PAST PARTICIPLE
averiguado

IMPERATIVE
averigua
averiguad

GERUND
averiguando

PRESENT

yo	averiguo
tú	averiguas
él	averigua
nosotros	averiguamos
vosotros	averiguáis
ellos	averiguan

FUTURE

yo	averiguaré
tú	averiguarás
él	averiguará
nosotros	averiguaremos
vosotros	averiguaréis
ellos	averiguarán

IMPERFECT

yo	averiguaba
tú	averiguabas
él	averiguaba
nosotros	averiguábamos
vosotros	averiguabais
ellos	averiguaban

PRESENT SUBJUNCTIVE

yo	averigüe
tú	averigües
él	avergüe
nosotros	averigüemos
vosotros	averigüéis
ellos	averigüen

CONDITIONAL

yo	averiguaría
tú	averiguarías
él	averiguaría
nosotros	averiguaríamos
vosotros	averiguaríais
ellos	averiguarían

PRETERITE

yo	averigüé
tú	averiguaste
él	averiguó
nosotros	averiguamos
vosotros	averiguasteis
ellos	averiguaron

bendecir *to bless*

PAST PARTICIPLE
bendec**ido**

GERUND
bendiciendo

IMPERATIVE
bendice
bendec**id**

PRESENT		*PRESENT SUBJUNCTIVE*	
yo	**bendigo**	yo	**bendiga**
tú	**bendices**	tú	**bendigas**
él	**bendice**	él	**bendiga**
nosotros	bendec**imos**	nosotros	**bendigamos**
vosotros	bendec**ís**	vosotros	**bendigáis**
ellos	**bendicen**	ellos	**bendigan**

FUTURE		*CONDITIONAL*	
yo	bendecir**é**	yo	bendecir**ía**
tú	bendecir**ás**	tú	bendecir**ías**
él	bendecir**á**	él	bendecir**ía**
nosotros	bendecir**emos**	nosotros	bendecir**íamos**
vosotros	bendecir**éis**	vosotros	bendecir**íais**
ellos	bendecir**án**	ellos	bendecir**ían**

IMPERFECT		*PRETERITE*	
yo	bendec**ía**	yo	**bendije**
tú	bendec**ías**	tú	**bendijiste**
él	bendec**ía**	él	**bendijo**
nosotros	bendec**íamos**	nosotros	**bendijimos**
vosotros	bendec**íais**	vosotros	**bendijisteis**
ellos	bendec**ían**	ellos	**bendijeron**

caber *to fit*

PAST PARTICIPLE
cabido

IMPERATIVE
cabe
cabed

GERUND
cabiendo

PRESENT		PRESENT SUBJUNCTIVE	
yo	quepo	yo	quepa
tú	cabes	tú	quepas
él	cabe	él	quepa
nosotros	cabemos	nosotros	quepamos
vosotros	cabéis	vosotros	quepáis
ellos	caben	ellos	quepan

FUTURE		CONDITIONAL	
yo	cabré	yo	cabría
tú	cabrás	tú	cabrías
él	cabrá	él	cabría
nosotros	cabremos	nosotros	cabríamos
vosotros	cabréis	vosotros	cabríais
ellos	cabrán	ellos	cabrían

IMPERFECT		PRETERITE	
yo	cabía	yo	cupe
tú	cabías	tú	cupiste
él	cabía	él	cupo
nosotros	cabíamos	nosotros	cupimos
vosotros	cabíais	vosotros	cupisteis
ellos	cabían	ellos	cupieron

caer *to fall*

PAST PARTICIPLE
caído

GERUND
cayendo

IMPERATIVE
cae
cae**d**

PRESENT	
yo	caigo
tú	caes
él	cae
nosotros	caemos
vosotros	caéis
ellos	caen

FUTURE	
yo	caeré
tú	caerás
él	caerá
nosotros	caeremos
vosotros	caeréis
ellos	caerán

IMPERFECT	
yo	caía
tú	caías
él	caía
nosotros	caíamos
vosotros	caíais
ellos	caían

PRESENT SUBJUNCTIVE	
yo	caiga
tú	caigas
él	caiga
nosotros	caigamos
vosotros	caigáis
ellos	caigan

CONDITIONAL	
yo	caería
tú	caerías
él	caería
nosotros	caeríamos
vosotros	caeríais
ellos	caerían

PRETERITE	
yo	caí
tú	caíste
él	cayó
nosotros	caímos
vosotros	caísteis
ellos	cayeron

cocer *to boil*

PAST PARTICIPLE	IMPERATIVE
cocido	**cuece**
	coced

GERUND
cociendo

PRESENT		PRESENT SUBJUNCTIVE	
yo	**cuezo**	yo	**cueza**
tú	**cueces**	tú	**cuezas**
él	**cuece**	él	**cueza**
nosotros	cocemos	nosotros	cozamos
vosotros	cocéis	vosotros	cozáis
ellos	**cuecen**	ellos	**cuezan**

FUTURE		CONDITIONAL	
yo	coceré	yo	cocería
tú	cocerás	tú	cocerías
él	cocerá	él	cocería
nosotros	coceremos	nosotros	coceríamos
vosotros	coceréis	vosotros	coceríais
ellos	cocerán	ellos	cocerían

IMPERFECT		PRETERITE	
yo	cocía	yo	cocí
tú	cocías	tú	cociste
él	cocía	él	coció
nosotros	cocíamos	nosotros	cocimos
vosotros	cocíais	vosotros	cocisteis
ellos	cocían	ellos	cocieron

coger to catch

PAST PARTICIPLE	IMPERATIVE
cog**ido**	coge
	cog**ed**

GERUND
cog**iendo**

PRESENT		PRESENT SUBJUNCTIVE	
yo	cojo	yo	coja
tú	coges	tú	cojas
él	coge	él	coja
nosotros	cogemos	nosotros	cojamos
vosotros	cogéis	vosotros	cojáis
ellos	cogen	ellos	cojan

FUTURE		CONDITIONAL	
yo	cogeré	yo	cogería
tú	cogerás	tú	cogerías
él	cogerá	él	cogería
nosotros	cogeremos	nosotros	cogeríamos
vosotros	cogeréis	vosotros	cogeríais
ellos	cogerán	ellos	cogerían

IMPERFECT		PRETERITE	
yo	cogía	yo	cogí
tú	cogías	tú	cogiste
él	cogía	él	cogió
nosotros	cogíamos	nosotros	cogimos
vosotros	cogíais	vosotros	cogisteis
ellos	cogían	ellos	cogieron

conducir *to drive, to lead*

PAST PARTICIPLE
conduc**ido**

IMPERATIVE
conduc**e**
conduc**id**

GERUND
conduc**iendo**

PRESENT	
yo	**conduzco**
tú	**conduces**
él	conduce
nosotros	conducimos
vosotros	conducís
ellos	conducen

FUTURE	
yo	conduciré
tú	conducirás
él	conducirá
nosotros	conduciremos
vosotros	conduciréis
ellos	conducirán

IMPERFECT	
yo	conducía
tú	conducías
él	conducía
nosotros	conducíamos
vosotros	conducíais
ellos	conducían

PRESENT SUBJUNCTIVE	
yo	**conduzca**
tú	**conduzcas**
él	**conduzca**
nosotros	**conduzcamos**
vosotros	**conduzcáis**
ellos	**conduzcan**

CONDITIONAL	
yo	conduciría
tú	conducirías
él	conduciría
nosotros	conduciríamos
vosotros	conduciríais
ellos	conducirían

PRETERITE	
yo	**conduje**
tú	**condujiste**
él	**condujo**
nosotros	**condujimos**
vosotros	**condujisteis**
ellos	**condujeron**

construir *to build*

PAST PARTICIPLE
construido

IMPERATIVE
construye
construid

GERUND
construyendo

PRESENT	
yo	**construyo**
tú	**construyes**
él	**construye**
nosotros	construimos
vosotros	construís
ellos	**construyen**

PRESENT SUBJUNCTIVE	
yo	**construya**
tú	**construyas**
él	**construya**
nosotros	**construyamos**
vosotros	**construyáis**
ellos	**construyan**

FUTURE	
yo	construiré
tú	construirás
él	construirá
nosotros	construiremos
vosotros	construiréis
ellos	construirán

CONDITIONAL	
yo	construiría
tú	construirías
él	construiría
nosotros	construiríamos
vosotros	construiríais
ellos	construirían

IMPERFECT	
yo	construía
tú	construías
él	construía
nosotros	construíamos
vosotros	construíais
ellos	construían

PRETERITE	
yo	construí
tú	construiste
él	**construyó**
nosotros	construimos
vosotros	construisteis
ellos	**construyeron**

contar to tell, to count

PAST PARTICIPLE
contado

IMPERATIVE
cuenta
contad

GERUND
contando

PRESENT		*PRESENT SUBJUNCTIVE*	
yo	cuento	yo	cuente
tú	cuentas	tú	cuentes
él	cuenta	él	cuente
nosotros	contamos	nosotros	contemos
vosotros	contáis	vosotros	contéis
ellos	cuentan	ellos	cuenten

FUTURE		*CONDITIONAL*	
yo	contaré	yo	contaría
tú	contarás	tú	contarías
él	contará	él	contaría
nosotros	contaremos	nosotros	contaríamos
vosotros	contaréis	vosotros	contaríais
ellos	contarán	ellos	contarían

IMPERFECT		*PRETERITE*	
yo	contaba	yo	conté
tú	contabas	tú	contaste
él	contaba	él	contó
nosotros	contábamos	nosotros	contamos
vosotros	contabais	vosotros	contasteis
ellos	contaban	ellos	contaron

crecer *to grow*

PAST PARTICIPLE	IMPERATIVE
crecido	crece
	creced

GERUND
creciendo

PRESENT		PRESENT SUBJUNCTIVE	
yo	crezco	yo	crezca
tú	creces	tú	crezcas
él	crece	él	crezca
nosotros	crecemos	nosotros	crezcamos
vosotros	crecéis	vosotros	crezcáis
ellos	crecen	ellos	crezcan

FUTURE		CONDITIONAL	
yo	creceré	yo	crecería
tú	crecerás	tú	crecerías
él	crecerá	él	crecería
nosotros	creceremos	nosotros	creceríamos
vosotros	creceréis	vosotros	creceríais
ellos	crecerán	ellos	crecerían

IMPERFECT		PRETERITE	
yo	crecía	yo	crecí
tú	crecías	tú	creciste
él	crecía	él	creció
nosotros	crecíamos	nosotros	crecimos
vosotros	crecíais	vosotros	crecisteis
ellos	crecían	ellos	crecieron

cruzar *to cross*

PAST PARTICIPLE
cruz**ado**

GERUND
cruz**ando**

IMPERATIVE
cruz**a**
cruz**ad**

PRESENT
yo	cruzo
tú	cruzas
él	cruza
nosotros	cruzamos
vosotros	cruzáis
ellos	cruzan

PRESENT SUBJUNCTIVE
yo	cruce
tú	cruces
él	cruce
nosotros	crucemos
vosotros	crucéis
ellos	crucen

FUTURE
yo	cruzaré
tú	cruzarás
él	cruzará
nosotros	cruzaremos
vosotros	cruzaréis
ellos	cruzarán

CONDITIONAL
yo	cruzaría
tú	cruzarías
él	cruzaría
nosotros	cruzaríamos
vosotros	cruzaríais
ellos	cruzarían

IMPERFECT
yo	cruzaba
tú	cruzabas
él	cruzaba
nosotros	cruzábamos
vosotros	cruzabais
ellos	cruzaban

PRETERITE
yo	crucé
tú	cruzaste
él	cruzó
nosotros	cruzamos
vosotros	cruzasteis
ellos	cruzaron

cubrir *to cover*

PAST PARTICIPLE	IMPERATIVE
cubierto	cubre
	cubrid

GERUND
cubr**iendo**

PRESENT		PRESENT SUBJUNCTIVE	
yo	cubro	yo	cubra
tú	cubres	tú	cubras
él	cubre	él	cubra
nosotros	cubrimos	nosotros	cubramos
vosotros	cubrís	vosotros	cubráis
ellos	cubren	ellos	cubran

FUTURE		CONDITIONAL	
yo	cubriré	yo	cubriría
tú	cubrirás	tú	cubrirías
él	cubrirá	él	cubriría
nosotros	cubriremos	nosotros	cubriríamos
vosotros	cubriréis	vosotros	cubriríais
ellos	cubrirán	ellos	cubrirían

IMPERFECT		PRETERITE	
yo	cubría	yo	cubrí
tú	cubrías	tú	cubriste
él	cubría	él	cubrió
nosotros	cubríamos	nosotros	cubrimos
vosotros	cubríais	vosotros	cubristeis
ellos	cubrían	ellos	cubrieron

dar *to give*

PAST PARTICIPLE
  da**do**

IMPERATIVE
  da
  da**d**

GERUND
  da**ndo**

PRESENT

yo	doy
tú	das
él	da
nosotros	damos
vosotros	dais
ellos	dan

PRESENT SUBJUNCTIVE

yo	dé
tú	des
él	dé
nosotros	demos
vosotros	deis
ellos	den

FUTURE

yo	daré
tú	darás
él	dará
nosotros	daremos
vosotros	daréis
ellos	darán

CONDITIONAL

yo	daría
tú	darías
él	daría
nosotros	daríamos
vosotros	daríais
ellos	darían

IMPERFECT

yo	daba
tú	dabas
él	daba
nosotros	dábamos
vosotros	dabais
ellos	daban

PRETERITE

yo	di
tú	diste
él	dio
nosotros	dimos
vosotros	disteis
ellos	dieron

decir *to say*

PAST PARTICIPLE
dicho

IMPERATIVE
di
de**cid**

GERUND
diciendo

PRESENT		*PRESENT SUBJUNCTIVE*	
yo	**digo**	yo	**diga**
tú	**dices**	tú	**digas**
él	**dice**	él	**diga**
nosotros	**decimos**	nosotros	**digamos**
vosotros	**decís**	vosotros	**digáis**
ellos	**dicen**	ellos	**digan**

FUTURE		*CONDITIONAL*	
yo	**diré**	yo	**diría**
tú	**dirás**	tú	**dirías**
él	**dirá**	él	**diría**
nosotros	**diremos**	nosotros	**diríamos**
vosotros	**diréis**	vosotros	**diríais**
ellos	**dirán**	ellos	**dirían**

IMPERFECT		*PRETERITE*	
yo	**decía**	yo	**dije**
tú	**decías**	tú	**dijiste**
él	**decía**	él	**dijo**
nosotros	**decíamos**	nosotros	**dijimos**
vosotros	**decíais**	vosotros	**dijisteis**
ellos	**decían**	ellos	**dijeron**

dirigir *to direct*

PAST PARTICIPLE
dirigido

GERUND
dirigiendo

IMPERATIVE
dirige
dirigid

PRESENT
yo	dirijo
tú	diriges
él	dirige
nosotros	dirigimos
vosotros	dirigís
ellos	dirigen

FUTURE
yo	dirigiré
tú	dirigirás
él	dirigirá
nosotros	dirigiremos
vosotros	dirigiréis
ellos	dirigirán

IMPERFECT
yo	dirigía
tú	dirigías
él	dirigía
nosotros	dirigíamos
vosotros	dirigíais
ellos	dirigían

PRESENT SUBJUNCTIVE
yo	dirija
tú	dirijas
él	dirija
nosotros	dirijamos
vosotros	dirijáis
ellos	dirijan

CONDITIONAL
yo	dirigiría
tú	dirigirías
él	dirigiría
nosotros	dirigiríamos
vosotros	dirigiríais
ellos	dirigirían

PRETERITE
yo	dirigí
tú	dirigiste
él	dirigió
nosotros	dirigimos
vosotros	dirigisteis
ellos	dirigieron

distinguir *to distinguish*

PAST PARTICIPLE
distingu**ido**

GERUND
distingu**iendo**

IMPERATIVE
distingu**e**
distingu**id**

PRESENT
yo	**distingo**
tú	distingu**es**
él	distingu**e**
nosotros	distingu**imos**
vosotros	distingu**ís**
ellos	distingu**en**

FUTURE
yo	distinguir**é**
tú	distinguir**ás**
él	distinguir**á**
nosotros	distinguir**emos**
vosotros	distinguir**éis**
ellos	distinguir**án**

IMPERFECT
yo	distingu**ía**
tú	distingu**ías**
él	distingu**ía**
nosotros	distingu**íamos**
vosotros	distingu**íais**
ellos	distingu**ían**

PRESENT SUBJUNCTIVE
yo	**distinga**
tú	**distingas**
él	**distinga**
nosotros	**distingamos**
vosotros	**distingáis**
ellos	**distingan**

CONDITIONAL
yo	distinguir**ía**
tú	distinguir**ías**
él	distinguir**ía**
nosotros	distinguir**íamos**
vosotros	distinguir**íais**
ellos	distinguir**ían**

PRETERITE
yo	distingu**í**
tú	distingu**iste**
él	distingu**ió**
nosotros	distingu**imos**
vosotros	distingu**isteis**
ellos	distingu**ieron**

dormir *to sleep*

PAST PARTICIPLE
dormido

IMPERATIVE
duerme
dormid

GERUND
durmiendo

PRESENT

yo	**duermo**
tú	**duermes**
él	**duerme**
nosotros	dormimos
vosotros	dormís
ellos	**duermen**

PRESENT SUBJUNCTIVE

yo	**duerma**
tú	**duermas**
él	**duerma**
nosotros	**durmamos**
vosotros	**durmáis**
ellos	**duerman**

FUTURE

yo	dormiré
tú	dormirás
él	dormirá
nosotros	dormiremos
vosotros	dormiréis
ellos	dormirán

CONDITIONAL

yo	dormiría
tú	dormirías
él	dormiría
nosotros	dormiríamos
vosotros	dormiríais
ellos	dormirían

IMPERFECT

yo	dormía
tú	dormías
él	dormía
nosotros	dormíamos
vosotros	dormíais
ellos	dormían

PRETERITE

yo	dormí
tú	dormiste
él	**durmió**
nosotros	dormimos
vosotros	dormisteis
ellos	**durmieron**

elegir *to choose*

PAST PARTICIPLE
  elegido

GERUND
  eligiendo

IMPERATIVE
  elige
  elegid

PRESENT

yo	**elijo**
tú	**eliges**
él	**elige**
nosotros	**elegimos**
vosotros	**elegís**
ellos	**eligen**

FUTURE

yo	**elegiré**
tú	**elegirás**
él	**elegirá**
nosotros	**elegiremos**
vosotros	**elegiréis**
ellos	**elegirán**

IMPERFECT

yo	**elegía**
tú	**elegías**
él	**elegía**
nosotros	**elegíamos**
vosotros	**elegíais**
ellos	**elegían**

PRESENT SUBJUNCTIVE

yo	**elija**
tú	**elijas**
él	**elija**
nosotros	**elijamos**
vosotros	**elijáis**
ellos	**elijan**

CONDITIONAL

yo	**elegiría**
tú	**elegirías**
él	**elegiría**
nosotros	**elegiríamos**
vosotros	**elegiríais**
ellos	**elegirían**

PRETERITE

yo	**elegí**
tú	**elegiste**
él	**eligió**
nosotros	**elegimos**
vosotros	**elegisteis**
ellos	**eligieron**

empezar *to begin*

PAST PARTICIPLE	*IMPERATIVE*
empez**ado**	**empieza**
	empeza**d**

GERUND
empez**ando**

PRESENT

yo	**empiezo**
tú	**empiezas**
él	**empieza**
nosotros	empez**amos**
vosotros	empez**áis**
ellos	**empiezan**

FUTURE

yo	empezar**é**
tú	empezar**ás**
él	empezar**á**
nosotros	empezar**emos**
vosotros	empezar**éis**
ellos	empezar**án**

IMPERFECT

yo	empez**aba**
tú	empez**abas**
él	empez**aba**
nosotros	empez**ábamos**
vosotros	empez**abais**
ellos	empez**aban**

PRESENT SUBJUNCTIVE

yo	**empiece**
tú	**empieces**
él	**empiece**
nosotros	emp**ecemos**
vosotros	emp**ecéis**
ellos	**empiecen**

CONDITIONAL

yo	empezar**ía**
tú	empezar**ías**
él	empezar**ía**
nosotros	empezar**íamos**
vosotros	empezar**íais**
ellos	empezar**ían**

PRETERITE

yo	**empecé**
tú	empez**aste**
él	**empezó**
nosotros	empez**amos**
vosotros	empez**asteis**
ellos	empez**aron**

entender *to understand*

PAST PARTICIPLE
entend**ido**

GERUND
entend**iendo**

IMPERATIVE
entiende
entend**ed**

PRESENT		*PRESENT SUBJUNCTIVE*	
yo	**entiendo**	yo	**entienda**
tú	**entiendes**	tú	**entiendas**
él	**entiende**	él	**entienda**
nosotros	entend**emos**	nosotros	entend**amos**
vosotros	entend**éis**	vosotros	entend**áis**
ellos	**entienden**	ellos	**entiendan**

FUTURE		*CONDITIONAL*	
yo	entender**é**	yo	entender**ía**
tú	entender**ás**	tú	entender**ías**
él	entender**á**	él	entender**ía**
nosotros	entender**emos**	nosotros	entender**íamos**
vosotros	entender**éis**	vosotros	entender**íais**
ellos	entender**án**	ellos	entender**ían**

IMPERFECT		*PRETERITE*	
yo	entend**ía**	yo	entend**í**
tú	entend**ías**	tú	entend**iste**
él	entend**ía**	él	entend**ió**
nosotros	entend**íamos**	nosotros	entend**imos**
vosotros	entend**íais**	vosotros	entend**isteis**
ellos	entend**ían**	ellos	entend**ieron**

enviar *to send*

PAST PARTICIPLE
enviado

GERUND
enviando

IMPERATIVE
envía
enviad

PRESENT

yo	envío
tú	envías
él	envía
nosotros	enviamos
vosotros	enviáis
ellos	envían

FUTURE

yo	enviaré
tú	enviarás
él	enviará
nosotros	enviaremos
vosotros	enviaréis
ellos	enviarán

IMPERFECT

yo	enviaba
tú	enviabas
él	enviaba
nosotros	enviábamos
vosotros	enviabais
ellos	enviaban

PRESENT SUBJUNCTIVE

yo	envíe
tú	envíes
él	envíe
nosotros	enviemos
vosotros	enviéis
ellos	envíen

CONDITIONAL

yo	enviaría
tú	enviarías
él	enviaría
nosotros	enviaríamos
vosotros	enviaríais
ellos	enviarían

PRETERITE

yo	envié
tú	enviaste
él	envió
nosotros	enviamos
vosotros	enviasteis
ellos	enviaron

erguir *to erect*

PAST PARTICIPLE
erguido

IMPERATIVE
yergue
erguid

GERUND
irguiendo

PRESENT		
yo	**yergo**	
tú	**yergues**	
él	**yergue**	
nosotros	**erguimos**	
vosotros	**erguís**	
ellos	**yerguen**	

PRESENT SUBJUNCTIVE		
yo	**yerga**	
tú	**yergas**	
él	**yerga**	
nosotros	**irgamos**	
vosotros	**irgáis**	
ellos	**yergan**	

FUTURE		
yo	**erguiré**	
tú	**erguirás**	
él	**erguirá**	
nosotros	**erguiremos**	
vosotros	**erguiréis**	
ellos	**erguirán**	

CONDITIONAL		
yo	**erguiría**	
tú	**erguirías**	
él	**erguiría**	
nosotros	**erguiríamos**	
vosotros	**erguiríais**	
ellos	**erguirían**	

IMPERFECT		
yo	**erguía**	
tú	**erguías**	
él	**erguía**	
nosotros	**erguíamos**	
vosotros	**erguíais**	
ellos	**erguían**	

PRETERITE		
yo	**erguí**	
tú	**erguiste**	
él	**irguió**	
nosotros	**erguimos**	
vosotros	**erguisteis**	
ellos	**irguieron**	

errar *to err*

PAST PARTICIPLE
er**rado**

IMPERATIVE
yerra
errad

GERUND
er**rando**

PRESENT	
yo	**yerro**
tú	**yerras**
él	**yerra**
nosotros	erramos
vosotros	erráis
ellos	**yerran**

PRESENT SUBJUNCTIVE	
yo	**yerre**
tú	**yerres**
él	**yerre**
nosotros	erremos
vosotros	erréis
ellos	**yerren**

FUTURE	
yo	erraré
tú	errarás
él	errará
nosotros	erraremos
vosotros	erraréis
ellos	errarán

CONDITIONAL	
yo	erraría
tú	errarías
él	erraría
nosotros	erraríamos
vosotros	erraríais
ellos	errarían

IMPERFECT	
yo	erraba
tú	errabas
él	erraba
nosotros	errábamos
vosotros	errabais
ellos	erraban

PRETERITE	
yo	erré
tú	erraste
él	erró
nosotros	erramos
vosotros	errasteis
ellos	erraron

escribir *to write*

PAST PARTICIPLE
escrito

IMPERATIVE
escrib**e**
escrib**id**

GERUND
escrib**iendo**

PRESENT			*PRESENT SUBJUNCTIVE*	
yo	escribo		yo	escriba
tú	escribes		tú	escribas
él	escribe		él	escriba
nosotros	escribimos		nosotros	escribamos
vosotros	escribís		vosotros	escribáis
ellos	escriben		ellos	escriban

FUTURE			*CONDITIONAL*	
yo	escribiré		yo	escribiría
tú	escribirás		tú	escribirías
él	escribirá		él	escribiría
nosotros	escribiremos		nosotros	escribiríamos
vosotros	escribiréis		vosotros	escribiríais
ellos	escribirán		ellos	escribirían

IMPERFECT			*PRETERITE*	
yo	escribía		yo	escribí
tú	escribías		tú	escribiste
él	escribía		él	escribió
nosotros	escribíamos		nosotros	escribimos
vosotros	escribíais		vosotros	escribisteis
ellos	escribían		ellos	escribieron

estar *to be*

PAST PARTICIPLE
est**ado**

IMPERATIVE
est**á**
est**ad**

GERUND
est**ando**

PRESENT

yo	est**oy**
tú	est**ás**
él	est**á**
nosotros	est**amos**
vosotros	est**áis**
ellos	est**án**

FUTURE

yo	estar**é**
tú	estar**ás**
él	estar**á**
nosotros	estar**emos**
vosotros	estar**éis**
ellos	estar**án**

IMPERFECT

yo	est**aba**
tú	est**abas**
él	est**aba**
nosotros	est**ábamos**
vosotros	est**abais**
ellos	est**aban**

PRESENT SUBJUNCTIVE

yo	est**é**
tú	est**és**
él	est**é**
nosotros	est**emos**
vosotros	est**éis**
ellos	est**én**

CONDITIONAL

yo	estar**ía**
tú	estar**ías**
él	estar**ía**
nosotros	estar**íamos**
vosotros	estar**íais**
ellos	estar**ían**

PRETERITE

yo	est**uve**
tú	est**uviste**
él	est**uvo**
nosotros	est**uvimos**
vosotros	est**uvisteis**
ellos	est**uvieron**

freír *to fry*

PAST PARTICIPLE	IMPERATIVE
frito	**fríe**
	freíd

GERUND
friendo

PRESENT

yo	**frío**
tú	**fríes**
él	**fríe**
nosotros	**freímos**
vosotros	**freís**
ellos	**fríen**

FUTURE

yo	freiré
tú	freirás
él	freirá
nosotros	freiremos
vosotros	freiréis
ellos	freirán

IMPERFECT

yo	freía
tú	freías
él	freía
nosotros	freíamos
vosotros	freíais
ellos	freían

PRESENT SUBJUNCTIVE

yo	**fría**
tú	**frías**
él	**fría**
nosotros	**friamos**
vosotros	**friáis**
ellos	**frían**

CONDITIONAL

yo	freiría
tú	freirías
él	freiría
nosotros	freiríamos
vosotros	freiríais
ellos	freirían

PRETERITE

yo	**freí**
tú	**freíste**
él	**frió**
nosotros	**freímos**
vosotros	**freísteis**
ellos	**frieron**

gruñir to grunt

PAST PARTICIPLE
gruñido

IMPERATIVE
gruñe
gruñid

GERUND
gruñendo

PRESENT		PRESENT SUBJUNCTIVE	
yo	gruño	yo	gruña
tú	gruñes	tú	gruñas
él	gruñe	él	gruña
nosotros	gruñimos	nosotros	gruñamos
vosotros	gruñís	vosotros	gruñáis
ellos	gruñen	ellos	gruñan

FUTURE		CONDITIONAL	
yo	gruñiré	yo	gruñiría
tú	gruñirás	tú	gruñirías
él	gruñirá	él	gruñiría
nosotros	gruñiremos	nosotros	gruñiríamos
vosotros	gruñiréis	vosotros	gruñiríais
ellos	gruñirán	ellos	gruñirían

IMPERFECT		PRETERITE	
yo	gruñía	yo	gruñí
tú	gruñías	tú	gruñiste
él	gruñía	él	gruñó
nosotros	gruñíamos	nosotros	gruñimos
vosotros	gruñíais	vosotros	gruñisteis
ellos	gruñían	ellos	gruñeron

haber *to have (auxiliary)*

PAST PARTICIPLE
habido

IMPERATIVE
not used

GERUND
habiendo

PRESENT		*PRESENT SUBJUNCTIVE*	
yo	he	yo	haya
tú	has	tú	hayas
él	ha	él	haya
nosotros	hemos	nosotros	hayamos
vosotros	habéis	vosotros	hayáis
ellos	han	ellos	hayan
FUTURE		*CONDITIONAL*	
yo	habré	yo	habría
tú	habrás	tú	habrías
él	habrá	él	habría
nosotros	habremos	nosotros	habríamos
vosotros	habréis	vosotros	habríais
ellos	habrán	ellos	habrían
IMPERFECT		*PRETERITE*	
yo	había	yo	hube
tú	habías	tú	hubiste
él	había	él	hubo
nosotros	habíamos	nosotros	hubimos
vosotros	habíais	vosotros	hubisteis
ellos	habían	ellos	hubieron

hacer *to do, to make*

PAST PARTICIPLE
hecho

IMPERATIVE
haz
hace**d**

GERUND
hac**iendo**

PRESENT	
yo	**hago**
tú	**haces**
él	hace
nosotros	**hacemos**
vosotros	hac**éis**
ellos	**hacen**

PRESENT SUBJUNCTIVE	
yo	**haga**
tú	**hagas**
él	**haga**
nosotros	**hagamos**
vosotros	**hagáis**
ellos	**hagan**

FUTURE	
yo	**haré**
tú	**harás**
él	**hará**
nosotros	**haremos**
vosotros	**haréis**
ellos	**harán**

CONDITIONAL	
yo	**haría**
tú	**harías**
él	**haría**
nosotros	**haríamos**
vosotros	**haríais**
ellos	**harían**

IMPERFECT	
yo	**hacía**
tú	**hacías**
él	**hacía**
nosotros	**hacíamos**
vosotros	**hacíais**
ellos	**hacían**

PRETERITE	
yo	**hice**
tú	**hiciste**
él	**hizo**
nosotros	**hicimos**
vosotros	**hicisteis**
ellos	**hicieron**

hay *there is, there are*

PAST PARTICIPLE
hab**ido**

IMPERATIVE
not used

GERUND
hab**iendo**

PRESENT
hay

PRESENT SUBJUNCTIVE
haya

FUTURE
habrá

CONDITIONAL
habría

IMPERFECT
había

PRETERITE
hubo

ir *to go*

PAST PARTICIPLE
ido

IMPERATIVE
ve
id

GERUND
yendo

PRESENT

yo	voy
tú	vas
él	va
nosotros	vamos
vosotros	vais
ellos	van

PRESENT SUBJUNCTIVE

yo	vaya
tú	vayas
él	vaya
nosotros	vayamos
vosotros	vayáis
ellos	vayan

FUTURE

yo	iré
tú	irás
él	irá
nosotros	iremos
vosotros	iréis
ellos	irán

CONDITIONAL

yo	iría
tú	irías
él	iría
nosotros	iríamos
vosotros	iríais
ellos	irían

IMPERFECT

yo	iba
tú	ibas
él	iba
nosotros	íbamos
vosotros	ibais
ellos	iban

PRETERITE

yo	fui
tú	fuiste
él	fue
nosotros	fuimos
vosotros	fuisteis
ellos	fueron

jugar *to play*

PAST PARTICIPLE
  jug**ado**

GERUND
  jug**ando**

IMPERATIVE
  juega
  jug**ad**

PRESENT

yo	**juego**
tú	**juegas**
él	**juega**
nosotros	jugamos
vosotros	jugáis
ellos	**juegan**

FUTURE

yo	jugaré
tú	jugarás
él	jugará
nosotros	jugaremos
vosotros	jugaréis
ellos	jugarán

IMPERFECT

yo	jugaba
tú	jugabas
él	jugaba
nosotros	jugábamos
vosotros	jugabais
ellos	jugaban

PRESENT SUBJUNCTIVE

yo	**juegue**
tú	**juegues**
él	**juegue**
nosotros	**juguemos**
vosotros	**juguéis**
ellos	**jueguen**

CONDITIONAL

yo	jugaría
tú	jugarías
él	jugaría
nosotros	jugaríamos
vosotros	jugaríais
ellos	jugarían

PRETERITE

yo	**jugué**
tú	jugaste
él	jugó
nosotros	jugamos
vosotros	jugasteis
ellos	jugaron

leer *to read*

PAST PARTICIPLE
leído

GERUND
leyendo

IMPERATIVE
lee
leed

PRESENT

yo	leo
tú	lees
él	lee
nosotros	leemos
vosotros	leéis
ellos	leen

FUTURE

yo	leeré
tú	leerás
él	leerá
nosotros	leeremos
vosotros	leeréis
ellos	leerán

IMPERFECT

yo	leía
tú	leías
él	leía
nosotros	leíamos
vosotros	leíais
ellos	leían

PRESENT SUBJUNCTIVE

yo	lea
tú	leas
él	lea
nosotros	leamos
vosotros	leáis
ellos	lean

CONDITIONAL

yo	leería
tú	leerías
él	leería
nosotros	leeríamos
vosotros	leeríais
ellos	leerían

PRETERITE

yo	leí
tú	leíste
él	leyó
nosotros	leímos
vosotros	leísteis
ellos	leyeron

llover *to rain*

PAST PARTICIPLE
llov**ido**

IMPERATIVE
not used

GERUND
llov**iendo**

PRESENT	*PRESENT SUBJUNCTIVE*
llueve	**llueva**

FUTURE	*CONDITIONAL*
llover**á**	llover**ía**

IMPERFECT	*PRETERITE*
llov**ía**	llov**ió**

lucir *to shine*

PAST PARTICIPLE
lucido

IMPERATIVE
luce
lucid

GERUND
luciendo

PRESENT		PRESENT SUBJUNCTIVE	
yo	**luzco**	yo	**luzca**
tú	**luces**	tú	**luzcas**
él	**luce**	él	**luzca**
nosotros	**lucimos**	nosotros	**luzcamos**
vosotros	**lucís**	vosotros	**luzcáis**
ellos	**lucen**	ellos	**luzcan**

FUTURE		CONDITIONAL	
yo	**luciré**	yo	**luciría**
tú	**lucirás**	tú	**lucirías**
él	**lucirá**	él	**luciría**
nosotros	**luciremos**	nosotros	**luciríamos**
vosotros	**luciréis**	vosotros	**luciríais**
ellos	**lucirán**	ellos	**lucirían**

IMPERFECT		PRETERITE	
yo	**lucía**	yo	**lucí**
tú	**lucías**	tú	**luciste**
él	**lucía**	él	**lució**
nosotros	**lucíamos**	nosotros	**lucimos**
vosotros	**lucíais**	vosotros	**lucisteis**
ellos	**lucían**	ellos	**lucieron**

morir to die

PAST PARTICIPLE
muerto

IMPERATIVE
muere
morid

GERUND
muriendo

PRESENT

yo	**muero**
tú	**mueres**
él	**muere**
nosotros	**morimos**
vosotros	**morís**
ellos	**mueren**

PRESENT SUBJUNCTIVE

yo	**muera**
tú	**mueras**
él	**muera**
nosotros	**muramos**
vosotros	**muráis**
ellos	**mueran**

FUTURE

yo	**moriré**
tú	**morirás**
él	**morirá**
nosotros	**moriremos**
vosotros	**moriréis**
ellos	**morirán**

CONDITIONAL

yo	**moriría**
tú	**morirías**
él	**moriría**
nosotros	**moriríamos**
vosotros	**moriríais**
ellos	**morirían**

IMPERFECT

yo	**moría**
tú	**morías**
él	**moría**
nosotros	**moríamos**
vosotros	**moríais**
ellos	**morían**

PRETERITE

yo	**morí**
tú	**moriste**
él	**murió**
nosotros	**morimos**
vosotros	**moristeis**
ellos	**murieron**

mover *to move*

PAST PARTICIPLE
movido

IMPERATIVE
mueve
moved

GERUND
moviendo

PRESENT		PRESENT SUBJUNCTIVE	
yo	**muevo**	yo	**mueva**
tú	**mueves**	tú	**muevas**
él	**mueve**	él	**mueva**
nosotros	movemos	nosotros	movamos
vosotros	movéis	vosotros	mováis
ellos	**mueven**	ellos	**muevan**

FUTURE		CONDITIONAL	
yo	moveré	yo	movería
tú	moverás	tú	moverías
él	moverá	él	movería
nosotros	moveremos	nosotros	moveríamos
vosotros	moveréis	vosotros	moveríais
ellos	moverán	ellos	moverían

IMPERFECT		PRETERITE	
yo	movía	yo	moví
tú	movías	tú	moviste
él	movía	él	movió
nosotros	movíamos	nosotros	movimos
vosotros	movíais	vosotros	movisteis
ellos	movían	ellos	movieron

nacer *to be born*

PAST PARTICIPLE	IMPERATIVE
nacido	nace
	naced

GERUND
naciendo

PRESENT		PRESENT SUBJUNCTIVE	
yo	nazco	yo	nazca
tú	naces	tú	nazcas
él	nace	él	nazca
nosotros	nacemos	nosotros	nazcamos
vosotros	nacéis	vosotros	nazcáis
ellos	nacen	ellos	nazcan

FUTURE		CONDITIONAL	
yo	naceré	yo	nacería
tú	nacerás	tú	nacerías
él	nacerá	él	nacería
nosotros	naceremos	nosotros	naceríamos
vosotros	naceréis	vosotros	naceríais
ellos	nacerán	ellos	nacerían

IMPERFECT		PRETERITE	
yo	nacía	yo	nací
tú	nacías	tú	naciste
él	nacía	él	nació
nosotros	nacíamos	nosotros	nacimos
vosotros	nacíais	vosotros	nacisteis
ellos	nacían	ellos	nacieron

negar *to deny*

PAST PARTICIPLE
negado

GERUND
negando

IMPERATIVE
niega
negad

PRESENT
yo	niego
tú	niegas
él	niega
nosotros	negamos
vosotros	negáis
ellos	niegan

FUTURE
yo	negaré
tú	negarás
él	negará
nosotros	negaremos
vosotros	negaréis
ellos	negarán

IMPERFECT
yo	negaba
tú	negabas
él	negaba
nosotros	negábamos
vosotros	negabais
ellos	negaban

PRESENT SUBJUNCTIVE
yo	niegue
tú	niegues
él	niegue
nosotros	neguemos
vosotros	neguéis
ellos	nieguen

CONDITIONAL
yo	negaría
tú	negarías
él	negaría
nosotros	negaríamos
vosotros	negaríais
ellos	negarían

PRETERITE
yo	negué
tú	negaste
él	negó
nosotros	negamos
vosotros	negasteis
ellos	negaron

oír *to hear*

PAST PARTICIPLE	IMPERATIVE
oído	**oye**
	oíd

GERUND
oyendo

PRESENT		PRESENT SUBJUNCTIVE	
yo	oigo	yo	oiga
tú	oyes	tú	oigas
él	oye	él	oiga
nosotros	oímos	nosotros	oigamos
vosotros	oís	vosotros	oigáis
ellos	oyen	ellos	oigan

FUTURE		CONDITIONAL	
yo	oiré	yo	oiría
tú	oirás	tú	oirías
él	oirá	él	oiría
nosotros	oiremos	nosotros	oiríamos
vosotros	oiréis	vosotros	oiríais
ellos	oirán	ellos	oirían

IMPERFECT		PRETERITE	
yo	oía	yo	oí
tú	oías	tú	oíste
él	oía	él	oyó
nosotros	oíamos	nosotros	oímos
vosotros	oíais	vosotros	oísteis
ellos	oían	ellos	oyeron

oler *to smell*

PAST PARTICIPLE
  ol**ido**

IMPERATIVE
  huele
  ol**ed**

GERUND
  ol**iendo**

PRESENT
yo	**huelo**
tú	**hueles**
él	**huele**
nosotros	ol**emos**
vosotros	ol**éis**
ellos	**huelen**

PRESENT SUBJUNCTIVE
yo	**huela**
tú	**huelas**
él	**huela**
nosotros	ol**amos**
vosotros	ol**áis**
ellos	**huelan**

FUTURE
yo	oler**é**
tú	oler**ás**
él	oler**á**
nosotros	oler**emos**
vosotros	oler**éis**
ellos	oler**án**

CONDITIONAL
yo	oler**ía**
tú	oler**ías**
él	oler**ía**
nosotros	oler**íamos**
vosotros	oler**íais**
ellos	oler**ían**

IMPERFECT
yo	ol**ía**
tú	ol**ías**
él	ol**ía**
nosotros	ol**íamos**
vosotros	ol**íais**
ellos	ol**ían**

PRETERITE
yo	ol**í**
tú	ol**iste**
él	ol**ió**
nosotros	ol**imos**
vosotros	ol**isteis**
ellos	ol**ieron**

pagar *to pay*

PAST PARTICIPLE		IMPERATIVE	
pagado		paga	
		pagad	
GERUND			
pagando			

PRESENT		PRESENT SUBJUNCTIVE	
yo	pago	yo	pague
tú	pagas	tú	pagues
él	paga	él	pague
nosotros	pagamos	nosotros	paguemos
vosotros	pagáis	vosotros	paguéis
ellos	pagan	ellos	paguen

FUTURE		CONDITIONAL	
yo	pagaré	yo	pagaría
tú	pagarás	tú	pagarías
él	pagará	él	pagaría
nosotros	pagaremos	nosotros	pagaríamos
vosotros	pagaréis	vosotros	pagaríais
ellos	pagarán	ellos	pagarían

IMPERFECT		PRETERITE	
yo	pagaba	yo	pagué
tú	pagabas	tú	pagaste
él	pagaba	él	pagó
nosotros	pagábamos	nosotros	pagamos
vosotros	pagabais	vosotros	pagasteis
ellos	pagaban	ellos	pagaron

pedir *to ask for*

PAST PARTICIPLE
pedido

IMPERATIVE
pide
pedid

GERUND
pidiendo

PRESENT
yo	**pido**
tú	**pides**
él	**pide**
nosotros	**pedimos**
vosotros	**pedís**
ellos	**piden**

PRESENT SUBJUNCTIVE
yo	**pida**
tú	**pidas**
él	**pida**
nosotros	**pidamos**
vosotros	**pidáis**
ellos	**pidan**

FUTURE
yo	**pediré**
tú	**pedirás**
él	**pedirá**
nosotros	**pediremos**
vosotros	**pediréis**
ellos	**pedirán**

CONDITIONAL
yo	**pediría**
tú	**pedirías**
él	**pediría**
nosotros	**pediríamos**
vosotros	**pediríais**
ellos	**pedirían**

IMPERFECT
yo	**pedía**
tú	**pedías**
él	**pedía**
nosotros	**pedíamos**
vosotros	**pedíais**
ellos	**pedían**

PRETERITE
yo	**pedí**
tú	**pediste**
él	**pidió**
nosotros	**pedimos**
vosotros	**pedisteis**
ellos	**pidieron**

pensar *to think*

PAST PARTICIPLE	IMPERATIVE
pens**ado**	**piensa**
	pens**ad**
GERUND	
pens**ando**	

PRESENT		PRESENT SUBJUNCTIVE	
yo	**pienso**	yo	**piense**
tú	**piensas**	tú	**pienses**
él	**piensa**	él	**piense**
nosotros	pens**amos**	nosotros	pens**emos**
vosotros	pens**áis**	vosotros	pens**éis**
ellos	**piensan**	ellos	**piensen**

FUTURE		CONDITIONAL	
yo	pensar**é**	yo	pensar**ía**
tú	pensar**ás**	tú	pensar**ías**
él	pensar**á**	él	pensar**ía**
nosotros	pensar**emos**	nosotros	pensar**íamos**
vosotros	pensar**éis**	vosotros	pensar**íais**
ellos	pensar**án**	ellos	pensar**ían**

IMPERFECT		PRETERITE	
yo	pens**aba**	yo	pens**é**
tú	pens**abas**	tú	pens**aste**
él	pens**aba**	él	pens**ó**
nosotros	pens**ábamos**	nosotros	pens**amos**
vosotros	pens**abais**	vosotros	pens**asteis**
ellos	pens**aban**	ellos	pens**aron**

poder *to be able*

PAST PARTICIPLE
pod**ido**

IMPERATIVE
puede
pod**ed**

GERUND
pudiendo

PRESENT		*PRESENT SUBJUNCTIVE*	
yo	**puedo**	yo	**pueda**
tú	**puedes**	tú	**puedas**
él	**puede**	él	**pueda**
nosotros	**podemos**	nosotros	**podamos**
vosotros	**podéis**	vosotros	**podáis**
ellos	**pueden**	ellos	**puedan**

FUTURE		*CONDITIONAL*	
yo	**podré**	yo	**podría**
tú	**podrás**	tú	**podrías**
él	**podrá**	él	**podría**
nosotros	**podremos**	nosotros	**podríamos**
vosotros	**podréis**	vosotros	**podríais**
ellos	**podrán**	ellos	**podrían**

IMPERFECT		*PRETERITE*	
yo	**podía**	yo	**pude**
tú	**podías**	tú	**pudiste**
él	**podía**	él	**pudo**
nosotros	**podíamos**	nosotros	**pudimos**
vosotros	**podíais**	vosotros	**pudisteis**
ellos	**podían**	ellos	**pudieron**

poner to put

PAST PARTICIPLE	IMPERATIVE
puesto	pon
	poned
GERUND	
poniendo	

PRESENT		PRESENT SUBJUNCTIVE	
yo	pongo	yo	ponga
tú	pones	tú	pongas
él	pone	él	ponga
nosotros	ponemos	nosotros	pongamos
vosotros	ponéis	vosotros	pongáis
ellos	ponen	ellos	pongan
FUTURE		CONDITIONAL	
yo	pondré	yo	pondría
tú	pondrás	tú	pondrías
él	pondrá	él	pondría
nosotros	pondremos	nosotros	pondríamos
vosotros	pondréis	vosotros	pondríais
ellos	pondrán	ellos	pondrían
IMPERFECT		PRETERITE	
yo	ponía	yo	puse
tú	ponías	tú	pusiste
él	ponía	él	puso
nosotros	poníamos	nosotros	pusimos
vosotros	poníais	vosotros	pusisteis
ellos	ponían	ellos	pusieron

prohibir *to forbid*

PAST PARTICIPLE
prohib**ido**

IMPERATIVE
prohíbe
prohib**id**

GERUND
prohib**iendo**

PRESENT	
yo	prohíbo
tú	prohíbes
él	prohíbe
nosotros	prohibimos
vosotros	prohibís
ellos	prohíben

PRESENT SUBJUNCTIVE	
yo	prohíba
tú	prohíbas
él	prohíba
nosotros	prohibamos
vosotros	prohibáis
ellos	prohíban

FUTURE	
yo	prohibiré
tú	prohibirás
él	prohibirá
nosotros	prohibiremos
vosotros	prohibiréis
ellos	prohibirán

CONDITIONAL	
yo	prohibiría
tú	prohibirías
él	prohibiría
nosotros	prohibiríamos
vosotros	prohibiríais
ellos	prohibirían

IMPERFECT	
yo	prohibía
tú	prohibías
él	prohibía
nosotros	prohibíamos
vosotros	prohibíais
ellos	prohibían

PRETERITE	
yo	prohibí
tú	prohibiste
él	prohibió
nosotros	prohibimos
vosotros	prohibisteis
ellos	prohibieron

querer *to want*

PAST PARTICIPLE
que**rido**

IMPERATIVE
quiere
quer**ed**

GERUND
quer**iendo**

PRESENT		*PRESENT SUBJUNCTIVE*	
yo	quiero	yo	quiera
tú	quieres	tú	quieras
él	quiere	él	quiera
nosotros	queremos	nosotros	queramos
vosotros	queréis	vosotros	queráis
ellos	quieren	ellos	quieran

FUTURE		*CONDITIONAL*	
yo	querré	yo	querría
tú	querrás	tú	querrías
él	querrá	él	querría
nosotros	querremos	nosotros	querríamos
vosotros	querréis	vosotros	querríais
ellos	querrán	ellos	querrían

IMPERFECT		*PRETERITE*	
yo	quería	yo	quise
tú	querías	tú	quisiste
él	quería	él	quiso
nosotros	queríamos	nosotros	quisimos
vosotros	queríais	vosotros	quisisteis
ellos	querían	ellos	quisieron

rehusar *to refuse*

PAST PARTICIPLE
rehus**ado**

IMPERATIVE
rehú**sa**
rehus**ad**

GERUND
rehus**ando**

PRESENT

yo	rehú**so**
tú	rehú**sas**
él	rehú**sa**
nosotros	rehus**amos**
vosotros	rehus**áis**
ellos	rehú**san**

FUTURE

yo	rehusar**é**
tú	rehusar**ás**
él	rehusar**á**
nosotros	rehusar**emos**
vosotros	rehusar**éis**
ellos	rehusar**án**

IMPERFECT

yo	rehus**aba**
tú	rehus**abas**
él	rehus**aba**
nosotros	rehus**ábamos**
vosotros	rehus**abais**
ellos	rehus**aban**

PRESENT SUBJUNCTIVE

yo	rehú**se**
tú	rehú**ses**
él	rehú**se**
nosotros	rehus**emos**
vosotros	rehus**éis**
ellos	rehú**sen**

CONDITIONAL

yo	rehusar**ía**
tú	rehusar**ías**
él	rehusar**ía**
nosotros	rehusar**íamos**
vosotros	rehusar**íais**
ellos	rehusar**ían**

PRETERITE

yo	rehus**é**
tú	rehus**aste**
él	rehus**ó**
nosotros	rehus**amos**
vosotros	rehus**asteis**
ellos	rehus**aron**

reír *to laugh*

PAST PARTICIPLE
reído

GERUND
riendo

IMPERATIVE
ríe
reíd

PRESENT
yo	río
tú	ríes
él	ríe
nosotros	reímos
vosotros	reís
ellos	ríen

FUTURE
yo	reiré
tú	reirás
él	reirá
nosotros	reiremos
vosotros	reiréis
ellos	reirán

IMPERFECT
yo	reía
tú	reías
él	reía
nosotros	reíamos
vosotros	reíais
ellos	reían

PRESENT SUBJUNCTIVE
yo	ría
tú	rías
él	ría
nosotros	riamos
vosotros	riáis
ellos	rían

CONDITIONAL
yo	reiría
tú	reirías
él	reiría
nosotros	reiríamos
vosotros	reiríais
ellos	reirían

PRETERITE
yo	reí
tú	reíste
él	rió
nosotros	reímos
vosotros	reísteis
ellos	rieron

reñir *to scold*

PAST PARTICIPLE
reñ**ido**

GERUND
riñendo

IMPERATIVE
riñe
reñ**id**

PRESENT
yo	riño
tú	riñes
él	riñe
nosotros	reñimos
vosotros	reñís
ellos	riñen

FUTURE
yo	reñiré
tú	reñirás
él	reñirá
nosotros	reñiremos
vosotros	reñiréis
ellos	reñirán

IMPERFECT
yo	reñía
tú	reñías
él	reñía
nosotros	reñíamos
vosotros	reñíais
ellos	reñían

PRESENT SUBJUNCTIVE
yo	riña
tú	riñas
él	riña
nosotros	riñamos
vosotros	riñáis
ellos	riñan

CONDITIONAL
yo	reñiría
tú	reñirías
él	reñiría
nosotros	reñiríamos
vosotros	reñiríais
ellos	reñirían

PRETERITE
yo	reñí
tú	reñiste
él	riñó
nosotros	reñimos
vosotros	reñisteis
ellos	riñeron

resolver *to solve*

PAST PARTICIPLE
resuelto

IMPERATIVE
resuelve
resolv**ed**

GERUND
resolv**iendo**

PRESENT		*PRESENT SUBJUNCTIVE*	
yo	**resuelvo**	yo	**resuelva**
tú	**resuelves**	tú	**resuelvas**
él	**resuelve**	él	**resuelva**
nosotros	resolv**emos**	nosotros	resolv**amos**
vosotros	resolv**éis**	vosotros	resolv**áis**
ellos	**resuelven**	ellos	**resuelvan**

FUTURE		*CONDITIONAL*	
yo	resolver**é**	yo	resolver**ía**
tú	resolver**ás**	tú	resolver**ías**
él	resolver**á**	él	resolver**ía**
nosotros	resolver**emos**	nosotros	resolver**íamos**
vosotros	resolver**éis**	vosotros	resolver**íais**
ellos	resolver**án**	ellos	resolver**ían**

IMPERFECT		*PRETERITE*	
yo	resolv**ía**	yo	resolv**í**
tú	resolv**ías**	tú	resolv**iste**
él	resolv**ía**	él	resolv**ió**
nosotros	resolv**íamos**	nosotros	resolv**imos**
vosotros	resolv**íais**	vosotros	resolv**isteis**
ellos	resolv**ían**	ellos	resolv**ieron**

reunir *to put together, gather*

PAST PARTICIPLE
reunido

GERUND
reuniendo

IMPERATIVE
reúne
reunid

PRESENT

yo	reúno
tú	reúnes
él	reúne
nosotros	reunimos
vosotros	reunís
ellos	reúnen

FUTURE

yo	reuniré
tú	reunirás
él	reunirá
nosotros	reuniremos
vosotros	reuniréis
ellos	reunirán

IMPERFECT

yo	reunía
tú	reunías
él	reunía
nosotros	reuníamos
vosotros	reuníais
ellos	reunían

PRESENT SUBJUNCTIVE

yo	reúna
tú	reúnas
él	reúna
nosotros	reunamos
vosotros	reunáis
ellos	reúnan

CONDITIONAL

yo	reuniría
tú	reunirías
él	reuniría
nosotros	reuniríamos
vosotros	reuniríais
ellos	reunirían

PRETERITE

yo	reuní
tú	reuniste
él	reunió
nosotros	reunimos
vosotros	reunisteis
ellos	reunieron

rogar *to beg*

PAST PARTICIPLE
rog**ado**

IMPERATIVE
ruega
rog**ad**

GERUND
rog**ando**

PRESENT
yo	**ruego**
tú	**ruegas**
él	**ruega**
nosotros	rogamos
vosotros	rogáis
ellos	**ruegan**

FUTURE
yo	rogaré
tú	rogarás
él	rogará
nosotros	rogaremos
vosotros	rogaréis
ellos	rogarán

IMPERFECT
yo	rogaba
tú	rogabas
él	rogaba
nosotros	rogábamos
vosotros	rogabais
ellos	rogaban

PRESENT SUBJUNCTIVE
yo	**ruegue**
tú	**ruegues**
él	**ruegue**
nosotros	**roguemos**
vosotros	**roguéis**
ellos	**rueguen**

CONDITIONAL
yo	rogaría
tú	rogarías
él	rogaría
nosotros	rogaríamos
vosotros	rogaríais
ellos	rogarían

PRETERITE
yo	**rogué**
tú	rogaste
él	rogó
nosotros	rogamos
vosotros	rogasteis
ellos	rogaron

romper *to break*

PAST PARTICIPLE
roto

IMPERATIVE
rompe
romped

GERUND
rompiendo

PRESENT		*PRESENT SUBJUNCTIVE*	
yo	rompo	yo	rompa
tú	rompes	tú	rompas
él	rompe	él	rompa
nosotros	rompemos	nosotros	rompamos
vosotros	rompéis	vosotros	rompáis
ellos	rompen	ellos	rompan

FUTURE		*CONDITIONAL*	
yo	romperé	yo	rompería
tú	romperás	tú	romperías
él	romperá	él	rompería
nosotros	romperemos	nosotros	romperíamos
vosotros	romperéis	vosotros	romperíais
ellos	romperán	ellos	romperían

IMPERFECT		*PRETERITE*	
yo	rompía	yo	rompí
tú	rompías	tú	rompiste
él	rompía	él	rompió
nosotros	rompíamos	nosotros	rompimos
vosotros	rompíais	vosotros	rompisteis
ellos	rompían	ellos	rompieron

saber *to know*

PAST PARTICIPLE
sab**ido**

IMPERATIVE
sab**e**
sab**ed**

GERUND
sab**iendo**

PRESENT

yo	**sé**
tú	sab**es**
él	sab**e**
nosotros	sab**emos**
vosotros	sab**éis**
ellos	sab**en**

PRESENT SUBJUNCTIVE

yo	**sepa**
tú	**sepas**
él	**sepa**
nosotros	**sepamos**
vosotros	**sepáis**
ellos	**sepan**

FUTURE

yo	**sabré**
tú	**sabrás**
él	**sabrá**
nosotros	**sabremos**
vosotros	**sabréis**
ellos	**sabrán**

CONDITIONAL

yo	**sabría**
tú	**sabrías**
él	**sabría**
nosotros	**sabríamos**
vosotros	**sabríais**
ellos	**sabrían**

IMPERFECT

yo	sab**ía**
tú	sab**ías**
él	sab**ía**
nosotros	sab**íamos**
vosotros	sab**íais**
ellos	sab**ían**

PRETERITE

yo	**supe**
tú	**supiste**
él	**supo**
nosotros	**supimos**
vosotros	**supisteis**
ellos	**supieron**

sacar *to take out*

PAST PARTICIPLE	IMPERATIVE
sacado	saca
	sacad

GERUND
sacando

PRESENT		PRESENT SUBJUNCTIVE	
yo	saco	yo	saque
tú	sacas	tú	saques
él	saca	él	saque
nosotros	sacamos	nosotros	saquemos
vosotros	sacáis	vosotros	saquéis
ellos	sacan	ellos	saquen

FUTURE		CONDITIONAL	
yo	sacaré	yo	sacaría
tú	sacarás	tú	sacarías
él	sacará	él	sacaría
nosotros	sacaremos	nosotros	sacaríamos
vosotros	sacaréis	vosotros	sacaríais
ellos	sacarán	ellos	sacarían

IMPERFECT		PRETERITE	
yo	sacaba	yo	saqué
tú	sacabas	tú	sacaste
él	sacaba	él	sacó
nosotros	sacábamos	nosotros	sacamos
vosotros	sacabais	vosotros	sacasteis
ellos	sacaban	ellos	sacaron

salir *to go out*

PAST PARTICIPLE
sal**ido**

IMPERATIVE
sal
sal**id**

GERUND
sal**iendo**

PRESENT

yo	salgo
tú	sales
él	sale
nosotros	salimos
vosotros	salís
ellos	salen

FUTURE

yo	saldré
tú	saldrás
él	saldrá
nosotros	saldremos
vosotros	saldréis
ellos	saldrán

IMPERFECT

yo	salía
tú	salías
él	salía
nosotros	salíamos
vosotros	salíais
ellos	salían

PRESENT SUBJUNCTIVE

yo	salga
tú	salgas
él	salga
nosotros	salgamos
vosotros	salgáis
ellos	salgan

CONDITIONAL

yo	saldría
tú	saldrías
él	saldría
nosotros	saldríamos
vosotros	saldríais
ellos	saldrían

PRETERITE

yo	salí
tú	saliste
él	salió
nosotros	salimos
vosotros	salisteis
ellos	salieron

satisfacer *to satisfy*

PAST PARTICIPLE
satisfecho

IMPERATIVE
satisfaz/satisfa**ce**
satisfac**ed**

GERUND
satisfac**iendo**

PRESENT		PRESENT SUBJUNCTIVE	
yo	**satisfago**	yo	**satisfaga**
tú	**satisfaces**	tú	**satisfagas**
él	satisface	él	**satisfaga**
nosotros	satisfac**emos**	nosotros	**satisfagamos**
vosotros	satisfac**éis**	vosotros	**satisfagáis**
ellos	satisfac**en**	ellos	**satisfagan**

FUTURE		CONDITIONAL	
yo	**satisfaré**	yo	**satisfaría**
tú	**satisfarás**	tú	**satisfarías**
él	**satisfará**	él	**satisfaría**
nosotros	**satisfaremos**	nosotros	**satisfaríamos**
vosotros	**satisfaréis**	vosotros	**satisfaríais**
ellos	**satisfarán**	ellos	**satisfarían**

IMPERFECT		PRETERITE	
yo	satisfac**ía**	yo	**satisfice**
tú	satisfac**ías**	tú	**satisficiste**
él	satisfac**ía**	él	**satisfizo**
nosotros	satisfac**íamos**	nosotros	**satisficimos**
vosotros	satisfac**íais**	vosotros	**satisficisteis**
ellos	satisfac**ían**	ellos	**satisficieron**

seguir *to follow*

PAST PARTICIPLE
seguido

IMPERATIVE
sigue
seguid

GERUND
siguiendo

PRESENT
yo	**sigo**
tú	**sigues**
él	**sigue**
nosotros	**seguimos**
vosotros	**seguís**
ellos	**siguen**

FUTURE
yo	seguiré
tú	seguirás
él	seguirá
nosotros	seguiremos
vosotros	seguiréis
ellos	seguirán

IMPERFECT
yo	seguía
tú	seguías
él	seguía
nosotros	seguíamos
vosotros	seguíais
ellos	seguían

PRESENT SUBJUNCTIVE
yo	**siga**
tú	**sigas**
él	**siga**
nosotros	**sigamos**
vosotros	**sigáis**
ellos	**sigan**

CONDITIONAL
yo	seguiría
tú	seguirías
él	seguiría
nosotros	seguiríamos
vosotros	seguiríais
ellos	seguirían

PRETERITE
yo	seguí
tú	seguiste
él	**siguió**
nosotros	seguimos
vosotros	seguisteis
ellos	**siguieron**

sentir *to feel*

PAST PARTICIPLE
sent**ido**

IMPERATIVE
siente
sent**id**

GERUND
sintiendo

PRESENT
yo	**siento**
tú	**sientes**
él	**siente**
nosotros	sent**imos**
vosotros	sent**ís**
ellos	**sienten**

FUTURE
yo	sentir**é**
tú	sentir**ás**
él	sentir**á**
nosotros	sentir**emos**
vosotros	sentir**éis**
ellos	sentir**án**

IMPERFECT
yo	sent**ía**
tú	sent**ías**
él	sent**ía**
nosotros	sent**íamos**
vosotros	sent**íais**
ellos	sent**ían**

PRESENT SUBJUNCTIVE
yo	**sienta**
tú	**sientas**
él	**sienta**
nosotros	**sintamos**
vosotros	**sintáis**
ellos	**sientan**

CONDITIONAL
yo	sentir**ía**
tú	sentir**ías**
él	sentir**ía**
nosotros	sentir**íamos**
vosotros	sentir**íais**
ellos	sentir**ían**

PRETERITE
yo	sent**í**
tú	sent**iste**
él	s**i**nt**ió**
nosotros	sent**imos**
vosotros	sent**isteis**
ellos	s**i**nt**ieron**

ser *to be*

PAST PARTICIPLE
sido

IMPERATIVE
sé
sed

GERUND
siendo

PRESENT		*PRESENT SUBJUNCTIVE*	
yo	soy	yo	sea
tú	eres	tú	seas
él	es	él	sea
nosotros	somos	nosotros	seamos
vosotros	sois	vosotros	seáis
ellos	son	ellos	sean

FUTURE		*CONDITIONAL*	
yo	seré	yo	sería
tú	serás	tú	serías
él	será	él	sería
nosotros	seremos	nosotros	seríamos
vosotros	seréis	vosotros	seríais
ellos	serán	ellos	serían

IMPERFECT		*PRETERITE*	
yo	era	yo	fui
tú	eras	tú	fuiste
él	era	él	fue
nosotros	éramos	nosotros	fuimos
vosotros	erais	vosotros	fuisteis
ellos	eran	ellos	fueron

tener *to have*

PAST PARTICIPLE
ten**ido**

IMPERATIVE
ten
ten**ed**

GERUND
ten**iendo**

PRESENT			PRESENT SUBJUNCTIVE	
yo	tengo		yo	tenga
tú	tienes		tú	tengas
él	tiene		él	tenga
nosotros	tenemos		nosotros	tengamos
vosotros	tenéis		vosotros	tengáis
ellos	tienen		ellos	tengan

FUTURE			CONDITIONAL	
yo	tendré		yo	tendría
tú	tendrás		tú	tendrías
él	tendrá		él	tendría
nosotros	tendremos		nosotros	tendríamos
vosotros	tendréis		vosotros	tendríais
ellos	tendrán		ellos	tendrían

IMPERFECT			PRETERITE	
yo	tenía		yo	tuve
tú	tenías		tú	tuviste
él	tenía		él	tuvo
nosotros	teníamos		nosotros	tuvimos
vosotros	teníais		vosotros	tuvisteis
ellos	tenían		ellos	tuvieron

torcer *to twist*

PAST PARTICIPLE
torc**ido**

GERUND
torc**iendo**

IMPERATIVE
tuerce
torc**ed**

PRESENT

yo	**tuerzo**
tú	**tuerces**
él	**tuerce**
nosotros	torcemos
vosotros	torcéis
ellos	**tuercen**

FUTURE

yo	torceré
tú	torcerás
él	torcerá
nosotros	torceremos
vosotros	torceréis
ellos	torcerán

IMPERFECT

yo	torcía
tú	torcías
él	torcía
nosotros	torcíamos
vosotros	torcíais
ellos	torcían

PRESENT SUBJUNCTIVE

yo	**tuerza**
tú	**tuerzas**
él	**tuerza**
nosotros	**torzamos**
vosotros	**torzáis**
ellos	**tuerzan**

CONDITIONAL

yo	torcería
tú	torcerías
él	torcería
nosotros	torceríamos
vosotros	torceríais
ellos	torcerían

PRETERITE

yo	torcí
tú	torciste
él	torció
nosotros	torcimos
vosotros	torcisteis
ellos	torcieron

traer *to bring*

PAST PARTICIPLE	IMPERATIVE
traído	trae
	traed

GERUND
trayendo

PRESENT

yo	traigo
tú	traes
él	trae
nosotros	traemos
vosotros	traéis
ellos	traen

FUTURE

yo	traeré
tú	traerás
él	traerá
nosotros	traeremos
vosotros	traeréis
ellos	traerán

IMPERFECT

yo	traía
tú	traías
él	traía
nosotros	traíamos
vosotros	traíais
ellos	traían

PRESENT SUBJUNCTIVE

yo	traiga
tú	traigas
él	traiga
nosotros	traigamos
vosotros	traigáis
ellos	traigan

CONDITIONAL

yo	traería
tú	traerías
él	traería
nosotros	traeríamos
vosotros	traeríais
ellos	traerían

PRETERITE

yo	traje
tú	trajiste
él	trajo
nosotros	trajimos
vosotros	trajisteis
ellos	trajeron

valer to be worth

PAST PARTICIPLE
valido

IMPERATIVE
vale
valed

GERUND
valiendo

PRESENT		PRESENT SUBJUNCTIVE	
yo	valgo	yo	valga
tú	vales	tú	valgas
él	vale	él	valga
nosotros	valemos	nosotros	valgamos
vosotros	valéis	vosotros	valgáis
ellos	valen	ellos	valgan

FUTURE		CONDITIONAL	
yo	valdré	yo	valdría
tú	valdrás	tú	valdrías
él	valdrá	él	valdría
nosotros	valdremos	nosotros	valdríamos
vosotros	valdréis	vosotros	valdríais
ellos	valdrán	ellos	valdrían

IMPERFECT		PRETERITE	
yo	valía	yo	valí
tú	valías	tú	valiste
él	valía	él	valió
nosotros	valíamos	nosotros	valimos
vosotros	valíais	vosotros	valisteis
ellos	valían	ellos	valieron

vencer *to win*

PAST PARTICIPLE
vencido

IMPERATIVE
vence
venced

GERUND
venciendo

PRESENT		PRESENT SUBJUNCTIVE	
yo	venzo	yo	venza
tú	vences	tú	venzas
él	vence	él	venza
nosotros	vencemos	nosotros	venzamos
vosotros	vencéis	vosotros	venzáis
ellos	vencen	ellos	venzan

FUTURE		CONDITIONAL	
yo	venceré	yo	vencería
tú	vencerás	tú	vencerías
él	vencerá	él	vencería
nosotros	venceremos	nosotros	venceríamos
vosotros	venceréis	vosotros	venceríais
ellos	vencerán	ellos	vencerían

IMPERFECT		PRETERITE	
yo	vencía	yo	vencí
tú	vencías	tú	venciste
él	vencía	él	venció
nosotros	vencíamos	nosotros	vencimos
vosotros	vencíais	vosotros	vencisteis
ellos	vencían	ellos	vencieron

venir to come

PAST PARTICIPLE
ven**ido**

IMPERATIVE
ven
ven**id**

GERUND
viniendo

PRESENT		PRESENT SUBJUNCTIVE	
yo	vengo	yo	venga
tú	vienes	tú	vengas
él	viene	él	venga
nosotros	venimos	nosotros	vengamos
vosotros	venís	vosotros	vengáis
ellos	vienen	ellos	vengan

FUTURE		CONDITIONAL	
yo	vendré	yo	vendría
tú	vendrás	tú	vendrías
él	vendrá	él	vendría
nosotros	vendremos	nosotros	vendríamos
vosotros	vendréis	vosotros	vendríais
ellos	vendrán	ellos	vendrían

IMPERFECT		PRETERITE	
yo	venía	yo	vine
tú	venías	tú	viniste
él	venía	él	vino
nosotros	veníamos	nosotros	vinimos
vosotros	veníais	vosotros	vinisteis
ellos	venían	ellos	vinieron

ver *to see*

PAST PARTICIPLE **visto**	*IMPERATIVE* **ve** **ved**
GERUND **viendo**	

PRESENT		*PRESENT SUBJUNCTIVE*	
yo	**veo**	yo	**vea**
tú	**ves**	tú	**veas**
él	**ve**	él	**vea**
nosotros	**vemos**	nosotros	**veamos**
vosotros	**veis**	vosotros	**veáis**
ellos	**ven**	ellos	**vean**

FUTURE		*CONDITIONAL*	
yo	**veré**	yo	**vería**
tú	**verás**	tú	**verías**
él	**verá**	él	**vería**
nosotros	**veremos**	nosotros	**veríamos**
vosotros	**veréis**	vosotros	**veríais**
ellos	**verán**	ellos	**verían**

IMPERFECT		*PRETERITE*	
yo	**veía**	yo	**vi**
tú	**veías**	tú	**viste**
él	**veía**	él	**vio**
nosotros	**veíamos**	nosotros	**vimos**
vosotros	**veíais**	vosotros	**visteis**
ellos	**veían**	ellos	**vieron**

volcar to overturn

PAST PARTICIPLE
volc**ado**

GERUND
volc**ando**

IMPERATIVE
vuelca
volcad

PRESENT
yo	**vuelco**
tú	**vuelcas**
él	**vuelca**
nosotros	volcamos
vosotros	volcáis
ellos	**vuelcan**

FUTURE
yo	volcaré
tú	volcarás
él	volcará
nosotros	volcaremos
vosotros	volcaréis
ellos	volcarán

IMPERFECT
yo	volcaba
tú	volcabas
él	volcaba
nosotros	volcábamos
vosotros	volcabais
ellos	volcaban

PRESENT SUBJUNCTIVE
yo	**vuelque**
tú	**vuelques**
él	**vuelque**
nosotros	volquemos
vosotros	volquéis
ellos	**vuelquen**

CONDITIONAL
yo	volcaría
tú	volcarías
él	volcaría
nosotros	volcaríamos
vosotros	volcaríais
ellos	volcarían

PRETERITE
yo	volqué
tú	volcaste
él	volcó
nosotros	volcamos
vosotros	volcasteis
ellos	volcaron

volver to return

PAST PARTICIPLE
vuelto

GERUND
vol**viendo**

IMPERATIVE
vuelve
volv**ed**

PRESENT		PRESENT SUBJUNCTIVE	
yo	**vuelvo**	yo	**vuelva**
tú	**vuelves**	tú	**vuelvas**
él	**vuelve**	él	**vuelva**
nosotros	volvemos	nosotros	volvamos
vosotros	volvéis	vosotros	volváis
ellos	**vuelven**	ellos	**vuelvan**

FUTURE		CONDITIONAL	
yo	volveré	yo	volvería
tú	volverás	tú	volverías
él	volverá	él	volvería
nosotros	volveremos	nosotros	volveríamos
vosotros	volveréis	vosotros	volveríais
ellos	volverán	ellos	volverían

IMPERFECT		PRETERITE	
yo	volvía	yo	volví
tú	volvías	tú	volviste
él	volvía	él	volvió
nosotros	volvíamos	nosotros	volvimos
vosotros	volvíais	vosotros	volvisteis
ellos	volvían	ellos	volvieron

zurcir *to darn*

PAST PARTICIPLE
zurcido

GERUND
zurciendo

IMPERATIVE
zurce
zurcid

PRESENT
yo	zurzo
tú	zurces
él	zurce
nosotros	zurcimos
vosotros	zurcís
ellos	zurcen

PRESENT SUBJUNCTIVE
yo	zurza
tú	zurzas
él	zurza
nosotros	zurzamos
vosotros	zurzáis
ellos	zurzan

FUTURE
yo	zurciré
tú	zurcirás
él	zurcirá
nosotros	zurciremos
vosotros	zurciréis
ellos	zurcirán

CONDITIONAL
yo	zurciría
tú	zurcirías
él	zurciría
nosotros	zurciríamos
vosotros	zurciríais
ellos	zurcirían

IMPERFECT
yo	zurcía
tú	zurcías
él	zurcía
nosotros	zurcíamos
vosotros	zurcíais
ellos	zurcían

PRETERITE
yo	zurcí
tú	zurciste
él	zurció
nosotros	zurcimos
vosotros	zurcisteis
ellos	zurcieron

The following pages, 163 to 186, contain an index of over 2,800 commonly used verbs cross-referred to the appropriate conjugation model.

- Regular verbs belonging to the first, second and third conjugation are numbered 1, 2 and 3 respectively. For the regular conjugations see pp 6 to 13.

- Irregular verbs are numerically cross-referred to the appropriate model as conjugated on pp 82 to 161. Thus, **alzar** is cross-referred to p 100 where **cruzar**, the model for this verb group, is conjugated.

- Verbs which are most commonly used in the reflexive form — e.g. **amodorrarse** — have been cross-referred to the appropriate non-reflexive model. For the full conjugation of a reflexive verb, see pp 28 to 31.

- Verbs printed in **bold** — e.g. **abrir** — are themselves models.

- Superior numbers refer you to notes on p 187 which indicate how the verb differs from its model.

Notes

The notes below indicate special peculiarities of individual verbs.
When only some forms of a given tense are affected, all these are
shown. When all forms of the tense are affected, only the 1st and
2nd persons are shown, followed by *etc*.

1 Gerund *2* Past Participle *3* Present *4* Preterite *5* Present
Subjunctive *6* Imperfect Subjunctive

1) **acaecer, acontecer, amanecer, anochecer, competer,
   deshelar, escampar, granizar, helar, nevar, nublarse,
   relampaguear, tronar, verdear, verdecer:** used almost
   exclusively in infinitive and 3rd person singular
2) **asir** *3* asgo *5* asga, asgas *etc*
3) **atañer** *1* atañendo *4* atañó: see also 1) above
4) **balbucir** *3* balbuceo *5* balbucee, balbucees *etc*
5) **concernir** *3* concierne, conciernen *5* concierna, conciernan:
   only used in 3rd person
6) **degollar** *3* degüello, degüellas, degüella, degüellan *5* degüelle,
   degüelles, degüellen
7) **delinquir** *3* delinco *5* delinca, delincas *etc*
8) **desasir** *3* desasgo *5* desasga, desasgas *etc*
9) **discernir** *3* discierno, disciernes, discierne, disciernen *5*
   discierna, disciernas, disciernan
10) **enraizar** *3* enraízo, enraízas, enraíza, enraízan *5* enraíce,
    enraíces, enraícen
11) **pudrir** *2* podrido
12) **rehuir** *3* rehúyo, rehúyes, rehúye, rehúyen *5* rehúya, rehúyas,
    rehúyan
13) **roer** *4* royó, royeron *6* royera, royeras *etc*
14) **soler:** used only in present and imperfect indicative
15) **yacer** *3* yazgo *or* yazco *or* yago *5* yazga *etc or* yazca *etc or*
    yaga *etc*

The Gender of Nouns

In Spanish, all nouns are either masculine or feminine, whether denoting people, animals or things. Gender is largely unpredictable and has to be learnt for each noun. However, the following guidelines will help you determine the gender for certain types of nouns.

- Nouns denoting male people and animals are usually — but not always — masculine, e.g.

  un hombre   **un toro**
  a man   *a bull*
  un enfermero   **un semental**
  a (male) nurse   *a stallion*

- Nouns denoting female people and animals are usually — but not always — feminine, e.g.

  una niña   **una vaca**
  a girl   *a cow*
  una enfermera **una yegua**
  a nurse   *a mare*

- Some nouns are masculine *or* feminine depending on the sex of the person to whom they refer, e.g.

  un camarada   **una camarada**
  a (male) comrade   *a (female) comrade*
  un belga   **una belga**
  a Belgian (man)   *a Belgian (woman)*
  un marroquí   **una marroquí**
  a Moroccan (man)   *a Moroccan (woman)*

- Other nouns referring to either men or women have only one gender which applies to both, e.g.

  una persona   **una visita**
  a person   *a visitor*
  una víctima   **una estrella**
  a victim   *a star*

● Often the ending of a noun indicates its gender. Shown below are some of the most important to guide you.

Masculine endings

-o un clavo *a nail*, un plátano *a banana*
    EXCEPTIONS: **mano** *hand*, **foto** *photograph*, **moto(cicleta)** *motorbike*

-l un tonel *a barrel*, un hotel *a hotel*
    EXCEPTIONS: **cal** *lime*, **cárcel** *prison*, **catedral** *cathedral*, **col** *cabbage*, **miel** *honey*, **piel** *skin*, **sal** *salt*, **señal** *sign*

-r un tractor *a tractor*, el altar *the altar*
    EXCEPTIONS: **coliflor** *cauliflower*, **flor** *flower*, **labor** *task*

-y el rey *the king*, un buey *an ox*
    EXCEPTION: **ley** *law*

Feminine endings

-a una casa *a house*, la cara *the face*
    EXCEPTIONS: **día** *day*, **mapa** *map*, **planeta** *planet*, **tranvía** *tram*, and most words ending in -ma (**tema** *subject*, **problema** *problem*, etc)

-ión una canción *a song*, una procesión *a procession*
    EXCEPTIONS: most nouns not ending in -ción or -sión, e.g. **avión** *aeroplane*, **camión** *lorry*, **gorrión** *sparrow*

-dad, -tad, una ciudad *a town*, la libertad *freedom*, una
-tud multitud *a crowd*

-ed una pared *a wall*, la sed *thirst*
    EXCEPTION: **césped** *lawn*

-itis una faringitis *pharyngitis*, la celulitis *cellulitis*

-iz una perdiz *a partridge*, una matriz *a matrix*
    EXCEPTIONS: **lápiz** *pencil*, **maíz** *corn*, **tapiz** *tapestry*

-sis una tesis *a thesis*, una dosis *a dose*
    EXCEPTIONS: **análisis** *analysis*, **énfasis** *emphasis*, **paréntesis** *parenthesis*

-umbre la podredumbre *rot*, la muchedumbre *crowd*

Gender of nouns (contd)

Some nouns change meaning according to gender. The most common are set out below:

	MASCULINE	*FEMININE*	
capital	*capital* (money)	*capital* (city)	(→1)
clave	*harpsichord*	*clue*	
cólera	*cholera*	*anger*	(→2)
cometa	*comet*	*kite*	
corriente	*current month*	*current*	
corte	*cut*	*court* (royal)	(→3)
coma	*coma*	*comma*	(→4)
cura	*priest*	*cure*	(→5)
frente	*front* (in war)	*forehead*	(→6)
guardia	*guard(sman)*	*guard*	(→7)
guía	*guide* (person)	*guide(book)*	(→8)
moral	*mulberry tree*	*morals*	
orden	*order* (arrangement)	*order* (command)	(→9)
ordenanza	*office boy*	*ordinance*	
papa	*Pope*	*potato*	
parte	*dispatch*	*part*	(→10)
pendiente	*earring*	*slope*	
pez	*fish*	*pitch*	
policía	*policeman*	*police*	
radio	*radius, radium*	*radio*	

1 **Invirtieron mucho capital**
   They invested a lot of capital
   La capital es muy fea
   The capital city is very ugly

2 **Es difícil luchar contra el cólera**   **Montó en cólera**
   Cholera is difficult to combat   He got angry

3 **Me encanta tu corte de pelo**
   I love your haircut
   Se trasladó la corte a Madrid
   The court was moved to Madrid

4 **Entró en un coma profundo**
   He went into a deep coma
   Aquí hace falta una coma
   You need to put a comma here

5 **¿Quién es? — El cura**   **No tiene cura**
   Who is it? — The priest   It's hopeless

6 **Han mandado a su hijo al frente**
   Her son has been sent to the front
   Tiene la frente muy ancha
   She has a very broad forehead

7 **Vino un guardia de tráfico**
   A traffic policeman came
   Están relevando la guardia ahora
   They're changing the guard now

8 **Nuestro guía nos hizo reír a carcajadas**
   Our guide had us falling about laughing
   Busco una guía turística
   I'm looking for a guidebook

9 **Están en orden alfabético**
   They're in alphabetical order
   No hemos recibido la orden de pago
   We haven't had the payment order

10 **Le mandó un parte al general**
   He sent a dispatch to the general
   En alguna parte debe estar
   It must be somewhere or other

Gender: the formation of feminines

As in English, male and female are sometimes differentiated by the use of two quite separate words, e.g.

mi marido	**mi mujer**
my husband	*my wife*
un toro	**una vaca**
a bull	*a cow*

There are, however, some words in Spanish which show this distinction by the form of their ending

• Nouns ending in **-o** change to **-a** to form the feminine (→1)

• If the masculine singular form already ends in **-a**, no further **-a** is added to the feminine (→2)

• If the last letter of the masculine singular form is a consonant, an **-a** is normally added in the feminine* (→3)

Feminine forms to note

MASCULINE	FEMININE	
el abad	la abadesa	*abbot/abbess*
un actor	una actriz	*actor/actress*
el alcalde	la alcaldesa	*mayor/mayoress*
el conde	la condesa	*count/countess*
el duque	la duquesa	*duke/duchess*
el emperador	la emperatriz	*emperor/empress*
un poeta	una poetisa	*poet/poetess*
el príncipe	la princesa	*prince/princess*
el rey	la reina	*king/queen*
un sacerdote	una sacerdotisa	*priest/priestess*
un tigre	una tigresa	*tiger/tigress*
el zar	la zarina	*tzar/tzarina*

*If the last syllable has an accent, it disappears in the feminine (see p 292) (→4)

1 un amigo
   a (male) friend
   un empleado
   a (male) employee
   un gato
   a cat

una amiga
   a (female) friend
   una empleada
   a (female) employee
   una gata
   a (female) cat

2 un deportista
   a sportsman
   un colega
   a (male) colleague
   un camarada
   a (male) comrade

una deportista
   a sportswoman
   una colega
   a (female) colleague
   una camarada
   a (female) comrade

3 un español
   a Spaniard, a Spanish man
   un vendedor
   a salesman
   un jugador
   a (male) player

una española
   a Spanish woman
   una vendedora
   a saleswoman
   una jugadora
   a (female) player

4 un lapón
   a Laplander (man)
   un león
   a lion
   un neocelandés
   a New Zealander (man)

una lapona
   a Laplander (woman)
   una leona
   a lioness
   una neocelandesa
   a New Zealander (woman)

The formation of plurals

- Nouns ending in an unstressed vowel add **-s** to the singular form (→**1**)

- Nouns ending in a consonant or a stressed vowel add **-es** to the singular form (→**2**)

  EXCEPTIONS:

café	*coffee shop*	(plur: **cafés**)
mamá	*mummy*	(plur: **mamás**)
papá	*daddy*	(plur: **papás**)
pie	*foot*	(plur: **pies**)
sofá	*sofa*	(plur: **sofás**)
té	*tea*	(plur: **tes**)

  and words of foreign origin ending in a consonant, e.g.:

coñac	*brandy*	(plur: **coñacs**)
jersey	*jumper*	(plur: **jerseys**)

  It should be noted that:
  — nouns ending in **-n** or **-s** with an accent on the last syllable drop this accent in the plural (see p 292) (→**3**)
  — nouns ending in **-n** with the stress on the second-last syllable in the singular add an accent to that syllable in the plural in order to show the correct position for stress (see p 292) (→**4**)
  — nouns ending in **-z** change this to **c** in the plural (→**5**)

- Nouns with an unstressed final syllable ending in **-s** do not change in the plural (→**6**)

1 **la casa**
the house
el libro
the book

las casas
the houses
los libros
the books

2 **un rumor**
a rumour
un jabalí
a boar

unos rumores
(some) rumours
unos jabalíes
(some) boars

3 **la canción**
the song
el autobús
the bus

las canciones
the songs
los autobuses
the buses

4 **un examen**
an exam
un crimen
a crime

unos exámenes
(some) exams
unos crímenes
(some) crimes

5 **la luz**
the light

las luces
the lights

6 **un paraguas**
an umbrella
la dosis
the dose
el lunes
Monday

unos paraguas
(some) umbrellas
las dosis
the doses
los lunes
Mondays

The Definite Article

	WITH MASC NOUN	WITH FEM NOUN	
SING	el	la	the
PLUR	los	las	the

- The gender and number of the noun determine the form of the article (→1)

  It should be noted, however, that if the article comes directly before a feminine singular noun which starts with a stressed a- or ha-, the masculine form el is used instead of the feminine la (→2)

- For uses of the definite article see p 199

- a + el becomes al (→3)

- de + el becomes del (→4)

Continued

1 el tren   **la estación**
the train   the station
el actor   **la actriz**
the actor   the actress
los hoteles   **las escuelas**
the hotels   the schools
los profesores   **las mujeres**
the teachers   the women

2 el agua   *but*   **la misma agua**
the water   the same water
el hacha   *but*   **la mejor hacha**
the axe   the best axe

3 al cine
to the cinema
al empleado
to the employee
al hospital
to the hospital

4 del departamento
from/of the department
del autor
from/of the author
del presidente
from/of the president

Uses of the definite article

While the definite article is used in much the same way in Spanish as it is in English, its use is more widespread in Spanish. Unlike English the definite article is also used:

* with abstract nouns, except when following certain prepositions (→**1**)

* in generalizations, especially with plural or uncountable* nouns (→**2**)

* with parts of the body (→**3**)
  'Ownership' is often indicated by an indirect object pronoun or a reflexive pronoun (→**4**)

* with titles/ranks/professions followed by a proper name (→**5**)
  EXCEPTIONS: with **Don/Doña, San/Santo(a)** (→**6**)

* before nouns of official, academic and religious buildings, and names of meals and games (→**7**)

* The definite article is *NOT* used with nouns in apposition unless those nouns are individualized (→**8**)

*An uncountable noun is one which cannot be used in the plural or with an indefinite article, e.g. **el acero** *steel*, **la leche** *milk*.

1 Los precios suben
Prices are rising
El tiempo es oro
Time is money
but
con pasión   **sin esperanza**
with passion   without hope

2 No me gusta el café
I don't like coffee
Los niños necesitan ser queridos
Children need to be loved

3 Vuelva la cabeza hacia la izquierda
Turn your head to the left
No puedo mover las piernas
I can't move my legs

4 La cabeza me da vueltas
My head is spinning
Lávate las manos
Wash your hands

5 El rey Jorge III   **el capitán Menéndez**
King George III   Captain Menéndez
el doctor Ochoa   **el señor Ramírez**
Doctor Ochoa   Mr. Ramírez

6 Don Arturo Ruiz   **Santa Teresa**
Mr. Arturo Ruiz   Saint Teresa

7 en la cárcel   **en la universidad**   **en la iglesia**
in prison   at university   at church
la cena   **el tenis**   **el ajedrez**
dinner   tennis   chess

8 Madrid, capital de España, es la ciudad que …
Madrid, the capital of Spain, is the city which …
but
Maria Callas, la famosa cantante de ópera …
Maria Callas, the famous opera singer …

The Indefinite Article

	WITH MASC NOUN	WITH FEM NOUN	
SING	un	una	a
PLUR	unos	unas	some

The indefinite article is used in Spanish largely as it is in English EXCEPT:

- There is no article when a person's profession is being stated (→**1**)
  The article is used, however, when the profession is qualified by an adjective (→**2**)

- The article is not used with the following words:

otro	another	(→**3**)
cierto	certain	(→**4**)
semejante	such (a)	(→**5**)
tal	such (a)	(→**6**)
cien	a hundred	(→**7**)
mil	a thousand	(→**8**)
sin	without	(→**9**)
qué	what a	(→**10**)

- There is no article with a noun in apposition (→**11**). When an abstract noun is qualified by an adjective, the indefinite article is used, but is not translated in English (→**12**)

1 **Es profesor**   **Mi madre es enfermera**
  He's a teacher   My mother is a nurse
2 **Es un buen médico**
  He's a good doctor
  Se hizo una escritora célebre
  She became a famous writer
3 **otro libro**
  another book
4 **cierta calle**
  a certain street
5 **semejante ruido**
  such a noise
6 **tal mentira**
  such a lie
7 **cien soldados**
  a hundred soldiers
8 **mil años**
  a thousand years
9 **sin casa**
  without a house
10 **¡Qué sorpresa!**
  What a surprise!
11 **Baroja, gran escritor de la Generación del 98**
  Baroja, a great writer of the 'Generación del 98'
12 **con una gran sabiduría/un valor admirable**
  with great wisdom/admirable courage
  Dieron pruebas de una sangre fría increíble
  They showed incredible coolness
  una película de un mal gusto espantoso
  a film in appallingly bad taste

The Article 'lo'

This is never used with a noun. Instead, it is used in the following ways:

- As an intensifier before an adjective or adverb in the construction

  lo + adjective/adverb + **que** (→**1**)

  Note that the adjective agrees with the noun it refers to (→**2**)

- With an adjective or participle to form an abstract noun (→**3**)

- In the phrase **lo de** to refer to a subject of which speaker and listener are already aware. It can often be translated as *the business/affair of/about ...* (→**4**)

- In set expressions, the commonest of which are:

a lo mejor	*maybe, perhaps*	(→**5**)
a lo lejos	*in the distance*	(→**6**)
a lo largo de	*along, through*	(→**7**)
por lo menos	*at least*	(→**8**)
por lo tanto	*therefore, so*	(→**9**)
por lo visto	*apparently*	(→**10**)

1 **No sabíamos lo pequeña que era la casa**
We didn't know how small the house was
Sé lo mucho que te gusta la música
I know how much you like music

2 **No te imaginas lo simpáticos que son**
You can't imagine how nice they are
Ya sabes lo buenas que son estas manzanas
You already know how good these apples are

3 **Lo bueno de eso es que ...**
The good thing about it is that ...
Sentimos mucho lo ocurrido
We are very sorry about what happened

4 **Lo de ayer es mejor que lo olvides**
It's better if you forget what happened yesterday
Lo de tu hermano me preocupa mucho
The business about your brother worries me very much

5 **A lo mejor ha salido**
Perhaps he's gone out

6 **A lo lejos se veían unas casas**
Some houses could be seen in the distance

7 **A lo largo de su vida**
Throughout his life
A lo largo de la carretera
Along the road

8 **Hubo por lo menos cincuenta heridos**
At least fifty people were injured

9 **No hemos recibido ninguna instrucción al respecto, y por lo tanto no podemos ...**
We have not received any instructions about it, therefore we cannot ...

10 **Por lo visto, no viene**
Apparently he's not coming *or* He's not coming, it seems

Adjectives

Most adjectives agree in number and in gender with the noun or pronoun.

Note that:
- if the adjective refers to two or more singular nouns of the same gender, a plural ending of that gender is required (→1)
- if the adjective refers to two or more singular nouns of different genders, a masculine plural ending is required (→2)

The formation of feminines

- Adjectives ending in **-o** change to **-a** (→3)

- Some groups of adjectives add **-a**:
  - adjectives of nationality or geographical origin (→4)
  - adjectives ending in **-or** (except irregular comparatives: see p 210), **-án, -ón, -ín** (→5)
    Note: when there is an accent on the last syllable, it disappears in the feminine (see p 292)

- Other adjectives do not change (→6)

The formation of plurals

- Adjectives ending in an unstressed vowel add **-s** (→7)

- Adjectives ending in a stressed vowel or a consonant add **-es** (→8)
  Note that:
  - if there is an accent on the last syllable of a word ending in a consonant, it will disappear in the plural (see p 292) (→9)
  - if the last letter is a **z** it will become a **c** in the plural (→10)

1 **la lengua y la literatura españolas**
(the) Spanish language and literature

2 **Nunca había visto árboles y flores tan raros**
I had never seen such strange trees and flowers

3 **mi hermano pequeño**
my little brother

mi hermana pequeña
my little sister

4 **un chico español**
a Spanish boy

una chica española
a Spanish girl

el equipo barcelonés
the team from Barcelona

la vida barcelonesa
the Barcelona way of life

5 **un niño encantador**
a charming little boy

una niña encantadora
a charming little girl

un hombre holgazán
an idle man

una mujer holgazana
an idle woman

un gesto burlón
a mocking gesture

una sonrisa burlona
a mocking smile

un chico cantarín
a boy fond of singing

una chica cantarina
a girl fond of singing

6 **un final feliz**
a happy ending

una infancia feliz
a happy childhood

mi amigo belga
my Belgian (male) friend

mi amiga belga
my Belgian (female) friend

el vestido verde
the green dress

la blusa verde
the green blouse

7 **el último tren**
the last train

los últimos trenes
the last trains

una casa vieja
an old house

unas casas viejas
(some) old houses

8 **un médico iraní**
an Iranian doctor

unos médicos iraníes
(some) Iranian doctors

un examen fácil
an easy exam

unos exámenes fáciles
(some) easy exams

9 **un río francés**
a French river

unos ríos franceses
(some) French rivers

10 **un día feliz**
a happy day

unos días felices
(some) happy days

Invariable Adjectives

Some adjectives and other parts of speech when used adjectivally never change in the feminine or plural.
The commonest of these are:
— nouns denoting colour (→1)
— compound adjectives (→2)
— nouns used as adjectives (→3)

Shortening of Adjectives

- The following drop the final **-o** before a masculine singular noun:
  bueno *good* (→4)
  malo *bad*
  alguno* *some* (→5)
  ninguno* *none*
  uno *one* (→6)
  primero *first* (→7)
  tercero *third*
  postrero *last* (→8)

*Note that an accent is required to show the correct position for stress.

- **Grande** *big, great* is usually shortened to **gran** before a masculine *or* feminine singular noun (→9)

- **Santo** *Saint* changes to **San** except with saints' names beginning with **Do-** or **To-** (→10)

- **Ciento** *a hundred* is shortened to **cien** before a masculine *or* feminine plural noun (→11)

- **Cualquiera** drops the final **-a** before a masculine *or* feminine singular noun (→12)

1 **los vestidos naranja**
the orange dresses

2 **las chaquetas azul marino**
the navy blue jackets

3 **bebés probeta**   **mujeres soldado**
test-tube babies   women soldiers

4 **un buen libro**
a good book

5 **algún libro**
some book

6 **cuarenta y un años**
forty-one years

7 **el primer hijo**
the first child

8 **un postrer deseo**
a last wish

9 **un gran actor**   **una gran decepción**
a great actor   a great disappointment

10 **San Antonio**   **Santo Tomás**
Saint Anthony   Saint Thomas

11 **cien años**
a hundred years
cien millones
a hundred million

12 **cualquier día**   **a cualquier hora**
any day   any time

Comparatives and Superlatives

Comparatives

These are formed using the following constructions:

más ... (que)	*more ... (than)*	(→1)
menos ... (que)	*less ... (than)*	(→2)
tanto ... como	*as ... as*	(→3)
tan ... como	*as ... as*	(→4)
tan ... que	*so ... that*	(→5)

demasiado ...
bastante ... } para   *too ...*
suficiente ...   *enough ...* } *to*   (→6)
     enough ...

• 'Than' followed by a clause is translated by **de lo que** (→7)

Superlatives

These are formed using the following constructions:

el/la/los/las más ... (que)	*the most ... (that)*	(→8)
el/la/los/las menos ... (que)	*the least ... (that)*	(→9)

• After a superlative the preposition **de** is often translated as *in* (→10)

• The absolute superlative (*very, most, extremely* + adjective) is expressed in Spanish by **muy** + adjective, or by adding **-ísimo/a/os/as** to the adjective when it ends in a consonant, or to its stem (adjective minus final vowel) when it ends in a vowel (→11)
Note that it is sometimes necessary to change the spelling of the adjective when **-ísimo** is added, in order to maintain the same sound (see p 296) (→12)

Continued

1 una razón más seria
a more serious reason
Es más alto que mi hermano
He's taller than my brother

2 una película menos conocida
a less well known film
Luis es menos tímido que tú
Luis is less shy than you

3 Pablo tenía tanto miedo como yo
Paul was as frightened as I was

4 No es tan grande como creía
It isn't as big as I thought

5 El examen era tan difícil que nadie aprobó
The exam was so difficult that nobody passed

6 No tengo suficiente dinero para comprarlo
I haven't got enough money to buy it

7 Está más cansada de lo que parece
She is more tired than she seems

8 el caballo más veloz   **la casa más pequeña**
the fastest horse   the smallest house
los días más lluviosos   **las manzanas más maduras**
the wettest days   the ripest apples

9 el hombre menos simpático   **la niña menos habladora**
the least likeable man   the least talkative girl
los cuadros menos bonitos   **las camisas menos viejas**
the least attractive paintings   the least old shirts

10 la estación más ruidosa de Londres
the noisiest station in London

11 Este libro es muy interesante   **Tienen un coche rapidísimo**
This book is very interesting   They have an extremely fast car
Era facilísimo de hacer
It was very easy to make

12 Mi tío era muy rico   **Se hizo riquísimo**
My uncle was very rich   He became extremely rich
un león muy feroz   **un tigre ferocísimo**
a very ferocious lion   an extremely ferocious tiger

Comparatives and Superlatives (contd)

Adjectives with irregular comparatives/ superlatives

ADJECTIVE	COMPARATIVE	SUPERLATIVE
bueno	**mejor**	**el mejor**
good	*better*	*the best*
malo	**peor**	**el peor**
bad	*worse*	*the worst*
grande	**mayor**	**el mayor**
big	*or*	*or*
	más grande	**el más grande**
	bigger; older	*the biggest; the oldest*
pequeño	**menor**	**el menor**
small	*or*	*or*
	más pequeño	**el más pequeño**
	smaller; younger; lesser	*the smallest; the youngest; the least*

- The irregular comparative and superlative forms of **grande** and **pequeño** are used mainly to express:
  - age, in which case they come after the noun ($\rightarrow$**1**)
  - abstract size and degrees of importance, in which case they come before the noun ($\rightarrow$**2**)

  The regular forms are used mainly to express physical size ($\rightarrow$**3**)

- Irregular comparatives and superlatives have one form for both masculine and feminine, but always agree in number with the noun ($\rightarrow$**1**)

1 mis hermanos mayores
my older brothers
la hija menor
the youngest daughter

2 el menor ruido
the slightest sound
las mayores dificultades
the biggest difficulties

3 Este plato es más grande que aquél
This plate is bigger than that one
Mi casa es más pequeña que la tuya
My house is smaller than yours

Demonstrative Adjectives

	MASCULINE	FEMININE	
SING	este	esta	this
	ese	esa	} that
	aquel	aquella	
PLUR	estos	estas	these
	esos	esas	} those
	aquellos	aquellas	

- Demonstrative adjectives normally precede the noun and always agree in number and in gender (→1)

- The forms **ese/a/os/as** are used:
  - to indicate distance from the speaker but proximity to the person addressed (→2)
  - to indicate a not too remote distance (→3)

- The forms **aquel/la/los/las** are used to indicate distance, in space or time (→4)

Examples ADJECTIVES **213**

1 Este bolígrafo no escribe
This pen is not working
Esa revista es muy mala
That is a very bad magazine
Aquella montaña es muy alta
That mountain (over there) is very high
¿Conoces a esos señores?
Do you know those gentlemen?
Siga Vd hasta aquellos edificios
Carry on until you come to those buildings
¿Ves aquellas personas?
Can you see those people (over there)?

2 Ese papel en donde escribes ...
That paper you are writing on ...

3 No me gustan esos cuadros
I don't like those pictures

4 Aquella calle parece muy ancha
That street (over there) looks very wide
Aquellos años sí que fueron felices
Those were really happy years

Interrogative Adjectives

	MASCULINE	FEMININE	
SING	{ ¿qué?	¿qué?	what?, which?
	{ ¿cuánto?	¿cuánta?	how much?; how many?
PLUR	{ ¿qué?	¿qué?	what?, which?
	{ ¿cuántos?	¿cuántas?	how much?; how many?

- Interrogative adjectives, when not invariable, agree in number and gender with the noun (→1)

- The forms shown above are also used in indirect questions (→2)

Exclamatory Adjectives

	MASCULINE	FEMININE	
SING	{ ¡qué!	¡qué!	what (a)
	{ ¡cuánto!	¡cuánta!	what (a lot of)
PLUR	{ ¡qué!	¡qué!	what
	{ ¡cuántos!	¡cuántas!	what (a lot of)

- Exclamatory adjectives, when not invariable, agree in number and gender with the noun (→3)

1 ¿Qué libro te gustó más?
Which book did you like most?
¿Qué clase de hombre es?
What type of man is he?
¿Qué instrumentos toca Vd?
What instruments do you play?
¿Qué ofertas ha recibido Vd?
What offers have you received?
¿Cuánto dinero te queda?
How much money have you got left?
¿Cuánta lluvia ha caído?
How much rain have we had?
¿Cuántos vestidos quieres comprar?
How many dresses do you want to buy?
¿Cuántas personas van a venir?
How many people are coming?

2 No sé a qué hora llegó
I don't know at what time she arrived
Dígame cuántas postales quiere
Tell me how many postcards you'd like

3 ¡Qué pena!
What a pity!
¡Qué tiempo tan/más malo!
What lousy weather!
¡Cuánto tiempo!
What a long time!
¡Cuánta pobreza!
What poverty!
¡Cuántos autobuses!
What a lot of buses!
¡Cuántas mentiras!
What a lot of lies!

Possessive Adjectives

Weak forms

WITH SING NOUN		WITH PLUR NOUN		
MASC	FEM	MASC	FEM	
mi	mi	mis	mis	my
tu	tu	tus	tus	your
su	su	sus	sus	his; her; its; your (of Vd)
nuestro	nuestra	nuestros	nuestras	our
vuestro	vuestra	vuestros	vuestras	your
su	su	sus	sus	their; your (of Vds)

- All possessive adjectives agree in number and (when applicable) in gender with the noun, NOT WITH THE OWNER (→1)

- The weak forms always precede the noun (→1)

- Since the form su(s) can mean his, her, your (of Vd, Vds) or their, clarification is often needed. This is done by adding de él, de ella, de Vds etc to the noun, and usually (but not always) changing the possessive to a definite article (→2)

Continued

1 Pilar no ha traído nuestros libros
Pilar hasn't brought our books
Antonio irá a vuestra casa
Anthony will go to your house
¿Han vendido su coche tus vecinos?
Have your neighbours sold their car?
Mi hermano y tu primo no se llevan bien
My brother and your cousin don't get on

2 su casa → la casa de él
his house
sus amigos → los amigos de Vd
your friends
sus coches → los coches de ellos
their cars
su abrigo → el abrigo de ella
her coat

Possessive Adjectives (contd)

Strong forms

WITH SING NOUN		WITH PLUR NOUN		
MASC	FEM	MASC	FEM	
mío	mía	míos	mías	my
tuyo	tuya	tuyos	tuyas	your
suyo	suya	suyos	suyas	his; her; its; your (of **Vd**)
nuestro	nuestra	nuestros	nuestras	our
vuestro	vuestra	vuestros	vuestras	your
suyo	suya	suyos	suyas	their; your (of **Vds**)

- The strong forms agree in the same way as the weak forms (see p 216)

- The strong forms always follow the noun, and they are used:
  - to translate the English of mine, of yours, etc (→1)
  - to address people (→2)

1 Es un capricho suyo
It's a whim of hers
un amigo nuestro
a friend of ours
una revista tuya
a magazine of yours

2 Muy señor mío (in letters)
Dear Sir
hija mía
my daughter
¡Dios mío!
My God!
Amor mío
My love/Darling

Indefinite Adjectives

alguno(a)s	*some*
ambos(as)	*both*
cada	*each; every*
cierto(a)s	*certain; definite*
cualquiera, plur **cualesquiera**	*some; any*
los (las) demás	*the others; the remainder*
mismo(a)s	*same; -self*
mucho(a)s	*many; much*
ningún, ninguna	*any; no*
plur **ningunos, ningunas**	
otro(a)s	*other; another*
poco(a)s	*few; little*
tal(es)	*such (a)*
tanto(a)s	*so much; so many*
todo(a)s	*all; every*
varios(as)	*several; various*

Unless invariable, all indefinite adjectives agree in number and gender with the noun (→**1**)

* **alguno**
  Before a masculine singular noun it drops the final **-o** and adds an accent to show the correct position for stress (→**2**) (see also p 292)

* **ambos**
  Usually it is only used in written Spanish. The spoken language prefers the form **los dos/las dos** (→**3**)

* **cierto** and **mismo**
  They change their meaning according to their position in relation to the noun (see also **Position of Adjectives**, p 224) (→**4**)

* **cualquiera**
  It drops the final **-a** before a masculine *or* feminine noun (→**5**)

Continued

1 **el mismo día**   **las mismas películas**
the same day   the same films
mucha/poca gente   **mucho/poco dinero**
many/few people   much/little money

2 **algún día**   **alguna razón**
some day   some reason

3 **Me gustan los dos cuadros**
I like both pictures
¿Conoces a las dos enfermeras?
Do you know both nurses?

4 **cierto tiempo**   *but*   **éxito cierto**
a certain time   sure success
el mismo color   *but*   **en la iglesia misma**
the same colour   in the church itself

5 **cualquier casa**   *but*   **una revista cualquiera**
any house   any magazine

Indefinite Adjectives (contd)

- **ningún** is only used in negative sentences or phrases (→**1**)

- **otro**
  It is never preceded by an indefinite article (→**2**)

- **tal**
  It is never followed by an indefinite article (→**3**)

- **todo**
  It can be followed by a definite article, a demonstrative or possessive adjective or a place name (→**4**)

  EXCEPTIONS:
  - when **todo** in the singular means *any, every,* or *each* (→**5**)
  - in some set expressions (→**6**)

1 No es ninguna tonta
She's no fool
¿No tienes parientes? — No, ninguno
Haven't you any relatives? — No, none

2 ¿Me das otra manzana?
Will you give me another apple?
Prefiero estos otros zapatos
I prefer these other shoes

3 Nunca dije tal cosa
I never said such a thing

4 Estudian durante toda la noche
They study all night
Ha llovido toda esta semana
It has rained all this week
Pondré en orden todos mis libros
I'll sort out all my books
Lo sabe todo Madrid
All Madrid knows it

5 Podrá entrar toda persona que lo desee
Any person who wishes to enter may do so
but
Vienen todos los días
They come every day

6 de todos modos   a toda velocidad
anyway   at full/top speed
por todas partes
por todos lados
a/en todas partes   } everywhere
a/en todos lados

Position of Adjectives

- Spanish adjectives usually follow the noun (→**1, 2**)

- Note that when used figuratively or to express a quality already inherent in the noun, adjectives can precede the noun (→**3**)

- As in English, demonstrative, possessive (weak forms), numerical, interrogative and exclamatory adjectives precede the noun (→**4**)

- Indefinite adjectives also usually precede the noun (→**5**)
  But note that **alguno** *some* in negative expressions follows the noun (→**6**)

- Some adjectives can precede or follow the noun, but their meaning varies according to their position:

BEFORE NOUN		AFTER NOUN	
antiguo	former	old, ancient	(→**7**)
diferente	various	different	(→**8**)
grande	great	big	(→**9**)
medio	half	average	(→**10**)
mismo	same	-self, very/precisely	(→**11**)
nuevo	new, another, fresh	brand new	(→**12**)
pobre	poor (wretched)	poor (not rich)	(→**13**)
puro	sheer, mere	pure (clear)	(→**14**)
varios	several	various, different	(→**15**)
viejo	old (long known, etc)	old (aged)	(→**16**)

- Adjectives following the noun are linked by **y** (→**17**)

1 **la página siguiente**   **la hora exacta**
the following page   the right time

2 **una corbata azul**   **una palabra española**
a blue tie   a Spanish word

3 **un dulce sueño**
a sweet dream
un terrible desastre (all disasters are terrible)
a terrible disaster

4 **este sombrero**   **mi padre**   **¿qué hombre?**
this hat   my father   what man?

5 **cada día**   **otra vez**   **poco dinero**
every day   another time   little money

6 **sin duda alguna**
without any doubt

7 **un antiguo colega**   **la historia antigua**
a former colleague   ancient history

8 **diferentes capítulos**   **personas diferentes**
various chapters   different people

9 **un gran pintor**   **una casa grande**
a great painter   a big house

10 **medio melón**   **velocidad media**
half a melon   average speed

11 **la misma respuesta**   **yo mismo**   **eso mismo**
the same answer   myself   precisely that

12 **mi nuevo coche**   **unos zapatos nuevos**
my new car   (some) brand new shoes

13 **esa pobre mujer**   **un país pobre**
that poor woman   a poor country

14 **la pura verdad**   **aire puro**
the plain truth   fresh air

15 **varios caminos**   **artículos varios**
several ways/paths   various items

16 **un viejo amigo**   **esas toallas viejas**
an old friend   those old towels

17 **una acción cobarde y falsa**
a cowardly, deceitful act

Personal Pronouns

SUBJECT PRONOUNS

PERSON	SINGULAR	PLURAL
1st	**yo**	**nosotros**
	I	*we* (masc/masc + fem)
		nosotras
		we (all fem)
2nd	**tú**	**vosotros**
	you	*you* (masc/masc + fem)
		vosotras
		you (all fem)
3rd	**él**	**ellos**
	he; it	*they* (masc/masc + fem)
	ella	**ellas**
	she; it	*they* (all fem)
	usted (Vd)	**ustedes (Vds)**
	you	*you*

- Subject pronouns have a limited usage in Spanish. Normally they are only used:
  - for emphasis (→1)
  - for clarity (→2)
  EXCEPTIONS: **Vd** and **Vds** should always be used for politeness, whether they are otherwise needed or not (→3)
- *It* as subject and *they*, referring to things, are never translated into Spanish (→4)
- **tú/usted**
  As a general rule, you should use **tú** (or **vosotros**, if plural) when addressing a friend, a child, a relative, someone you know well, or when invited to do so. In all other cases, use **usted** (or **ustedes**)
- **nosotros/as; vosotros/as; él/ella; ellos/ellas**
  All these forms reflect the number and gender of the noun(s) they replace. **Nosotros, vosotros** and **ellos** also replace a combination of masculine and feminine nouns.

Continued

1 Ellos sí que llegaron tarde
They really did arrive late
Tú no tienes por qué venir
There is no reason for you to come
Ella jamás creería eso
She would never believe that

2 Yo estudio español pero él estudia francés
I study Spanish but he studies French
Ella era muy deportista pero él prefería jugar a las cartas
She was a sporty type but he preferred to play cards
Vosotros saldréis primero y nosotros os seguiremos
You leave first and we will follow you

3 Pase Vd por aquí
Please come this way
¿Habían estado Vds antes en esta ciudad?
Had you been to this town before?

4 ¿Qué es? — Es una sorpresa
What is it? — It's a surprise
¿Qué son? — Son abrelatas
What are they? — They are tin-openers

Personal Pronouns (contd)

DIRECT OBJECT PRONOUNS

PERSON	SINGULAR	PLURAL
1st	**me**	**nos**
	me	*us*
2nd	**te**	**os**
	you	*you*
3rd (masculine)	**lo**	**los**
	him; it; you	*them; you*
	(of Vd)	*(of Vds)*
(feminine)	**la**	**las**
	her; it; you	*them; you*
	(of Vd)	*(of Vds)*

• **lo** sometimes functions as a 'neuter' pronoun, referring to an idea or information contained in a previous statement or question. It is often not translated (→**1**)

Position of direct object pronouns

• In constructions other than the imperative affirmative, infinitive or gerund, the pronoun always comes before the verb (→**2**)
In the imperative affirmative, infinitive and gerund, the pronoun follows the verb and is attached to it. An accent is needed in certain cases to show the correct position for stress (see also p 292) (→**3**)
• Where an infinitive or gerund depends on a previous verb, the pronoun may be used either after the infinitive or gerund, or before the main verb (→**4**)
Note how this applies to reflexive verbs (→**4**)
• For further information, see Order of Object Pronouns, p 232

Reflexive Pronouns

These are dealt with under reflexive verbs, p 24.

Continued

1 ¿Va a venir María? — No lo sé
Is Maria coming? — I don't know
Hay que regar las plantas — Yo lo haré
The plants need watering — I'll do it
Habían comido ya pero no nos lo dijeron
They had already eaten, but they didn't tell us
Yo conduzco de prisa pero él lo hace despacio
I drive fast but he drives slowly

2 Te quiero
I love you
¿Las ve Vd?
Can you see them?
¿No me oyen Vds?
Can't you hear me?
Tu hija no nos conoce
Your daughter doesn't know us
No los toques
Don't touch them

3 Ayúdame   **Acompáñenos**
Help me   Come with us
Quiero decirte algo
I want to tell you something
Estaban persiguiéndonos
They were coming after us

4 Lo está comiendo or **Está comiéndolo**
She is eating it
Nos vienen a ver or **Vienen a vernos**
They are coming to see us
No quería levantarse or **No se quería levantar**
He didn't want to get up
Estoy afeitándome or **Me estoy afeitando**
I'm shaving

Personal Pronouns (contd)

	INDIRECT OBJECT PRONOUNS	
PERSON	*SINGULAR*	*PLURAL*
1st	**me**	**nos**
2nd	**te**	**os**
3rd	**le**	**les**

- The pronouns shown in the above table replace the preposition **a** + noun (→**1**)

Position of indirect object pronouns

- In constructions other than the imperative affirmative, the infinitive or the gerund, the pronoun comes before the verb (→**2**)

 In the imperative affirmative, infinitive and gerund, the pronoun follows the verb and is attached to it. An accent is needed in certain cases to show the correct position for stress (see also p 292) (→**3**)

- Where an infinitive or gerund depends on a previous verb, the pronoun may be used either after the infinitive or gerund, or before the main verb (→**4**)

- For further information, see **Order of Object Pronouns**, p 232.

Reflexive Pronouns

These are dealt with under reflexive verbs, p 24

Continued

1 Estoy escribiendo a Teresa → **Le estoy escribiendo**
I am writing to Teresa   I am writing to her
  Da de comer al gato   → **Dale de comer**
  Give the cat some food   Give it some food

2 Sofía os ha escrito   **¿Os ha escrito Sofía?**
Sophie has written to you   Has Sophie written to you?
  Carlos no nos habla
  Charles doesn't speak to us
  ¿Qué te pedían?
  What were they asking you for?
  No les haga caso Vd
  Don't take any notice of them

3 Respóndame Vd   **Díganos Vd la respuesta**
Answer me   Tell us the answer
  No quería darte la noticia todavía
  I didn't want to tell you the news yet
  Llegaron diciéndome que …
  They came telling me that …

4 Estoy escribiéndole or **Le estoy escribiendo**
I am writing to him/her
  Les voy a hablar or **Voy a hablarles**
  I'm going to talk to them

Personal Pronouns (contd)

Order of object pronouns

- When two object pronouns of different persons are combined, the order is: indirect before direct, i.e.

$$\left.\begin{array}{l} \text{me} \\ \text{te} \\ \text{nos} \\ \text{os} \end{array}\right\} \text{ before } \left\{\begin{array}{l} \text{lo} \\ \text{la} \\ \text{los} \\ \text{las} \end{array}\right. \quad (\rightarrow 1)$$

Note: When two 3rd person object pronouns are combined, the first (i.e. the indirect object pronoun) becomes **se** ($\rightarrow$2)

Points to note on object pronouns

- As **le/les** can refer to either gender, and **se** to either gender, singular or plural, sometimes clarification is needed. This is done by adding **a él** *to him*, **a ella** *to her*, **a Vd** *to you* etc to the phrase, usually after the verb ($\rightarrow$3)

- When a noun object precedes the verb, the corresponding object pronoun must be used too ($\rightarrow$4)

- Indirect object pronouns are often used instead of possessive adjectives with parts of the body or clothing to indicate 'ownership', and also in certain common constructions involving reflexive verbs (see also **The Indefinite Article**, p 198) ($\rightarrow$5)

- **Le** and **les** are often used in Spanish instead of **lo** and **los** when referring to people. Equally **la** is sometimes used instead of **le** when referring to a feminine person or animal, although this usage is considered incorrect by some speakers of Spanish ($\rightarrow$6)

Continued

1 Paloma os lo mandará mañana
Paloma is sending it to you tomorrow
¿Te los ha enseñado mi hermana?
Has my sister shown them to you?
No me lo digas
Don't tell me (that)
Todos estaban pidiéndotelo
They were all asking you for it
No quiere prestárnosla
He won't lend it to us

2 Se lo di ayer
I gave it to him/her/them yesterday

3 Le escriben mucho a ella
They write to her often
Se lo van a mandar pronto a ellos
They will be sending it to them soon

4 A tu hermano lo conozco bien
I know your brother well
A María la vemos algunas veces
We sometimes see María

5 La chaqueta le estaba ancha
His jacket was too loose
Me duele el tobillo
My ankle is aching
Se me ha perdido el bolígrafo
I have lost my pen

6 Le/lo encontraron en el cine
They met him at the cinema
Les/los oímos llegar
We heard them coming
Le/la escribimos una carta
We wrote a letter to her

Personal Pronouns (contd)

Pronouns after prepositions

- These are the same as the subject pronouns, except for the forms **mí** *me*, **ti** *you* (sing), and the reflexive **sí** *himself, herself, themselves, yourselves* (→**1**)

- **Con** *with* combines with **mí**, **ti** and **sí** to form
  conmigo *with me*   (→**2**)
  contigo *with you*
  consigo *with himself/herself etc*

- The following prepositions always take a subject pronoun:

entre	*between, among* (→**3**)
hasta **incluso** }	*even, including* (→**4**)
salvo **menos** }	*except* (→**5**)
según	*according to* (→**6**)

- These pronouns are used for emphasis, especially where contrast is involved (→**7**)

- **Ello** *it, that* is used after a preposition when referring to an idea already mentioned, but never to a concrete noun (→**8**)

- **A él, de él** NEVER contract (→**9**)

1 Pienso en ti
I think about you

Es para ella
This is for her

Volveréis sin nosotros
You'll come back without us

Hablaba para sí
He was talking to himself

2 Venid conmigo
Come with me

Lo trajeron consigo
They brought it/him with them

3 entre tú y ella
between you and her

4 Hasta yo puedo hacerlo
Even I can do it

5 todos menos yo
everybody except me

6 según tú
according to you

7 ¿A ti no te escriben?
Don't they write to you?

Me lo manda a mí, no a ti
She is sending it to me, not to you

8 Nunca pensaba en ello
He never thought about it

Por todo ello me parece que ...
For all those reasons it seems to me that ...

9 A él no lo conozco
I don't know him

¿Son para mí?
Are they for me?

Iban hacia ellos
They were going towards them

Volaban sobre vosotros
They were flying above you

but **¿Hablaron con vosotros?**
Did they talk to you?

No he sabido nada de él
I haven't heard from him

Indefinite Pronouns

algo	*something, anything*	(→**1**)
alguien	*somebody, anybody*	(→**2**)
alguno/a/os/as	*some, a few*	(→**3**)
cada uno/a	*each (one)*	(→**4**)
	everybody	
cualquiera	*anybody; any*	(→**5**)
los/las demás	*the others*	
	the rest	(→**6**)
mucho/a/os/as	*many; much*	(→**7**)
nada	*nothing*	(→**8**)
nadie	*nobody*	(→**9**)
ninguno/a	*none, not any*	(→**10**)
poco/a/os/as	*few; little*	(→**11**)
tanto/a/os/as	*so much; so many*	(→**12**)
todo/a/os/as	*all; everything*	(→**13**)
uno ... (el) otro	} *(the) one ... the other*	
una ... (la) otra		
unos ... (los) otros	} *some ... (the) others*	(→**14**)
unas ... (las) otras		
varios/as	*several*	(→**15**)

● algo, alguien, alguno

They can never be used after a negative. The appropriate negative pronouns are used instead: **nada, nadie, ninguno** (see also negatives, p 272) (→**16**)

1 **Tengo algo para ti**   **¿Viste algo?**
I have something for you   Did you see anything?

2 **Alguien me lo ha dicho**   **¿Has visto a alguien?**
Somebody said it to me   Have you seen anybody?

3 **Algunos de los niños ya sabían leer**
Some of the children could read already

4 **Le dió una manzana a cada uno**   **¡Cada uno a su casa!**
She gave each of them an apple   Everybody go home!

5 **Cualquiera puede hacerlo**
Anybody can do it
Cualquiera de las explicaciones es a valid one
Any of the explanations is a valid one

6 **Yo me fui, los demás se quedaron**
I went, the others stayed

7 **Muchas de las casas no tenían jardín**
Many of the houses didn't have a garden

8 **¿Qué tienes en la mano? — Nada**
What have you got in your hand? — Nothing

9 **¿A quién ves? — A nadie**
Who can you see? — Nobody

10 **¿Cuántas tienes? — Ninguna**
How many have you got? — None

11 **Había muchos cuadros, pero vi pocos que me gustaran**
There were many pictures, but I saw few I liked

12 **¿Se oía mucho ruido? — No tanto**
Was it very noisy? — Not so very

13 **Lo ha estropeado todo**   **Todo va bien**
He has spoiled everything   All is going well

14 **Unos cuestan 300 pesetas, los otros 400 pesetas**
Some cost 300 pesetas, the others 400 pesetas

15 **Varios de ellos me gustaron mucho**
I liked several of them very much

16 **Veo a alguien**   **No veo a nadie**
I can see somebody   I can't see anybody
Tengo algo que hacer   **No tengo nada que hacer**
I have something to do   I don't have anything to do

Relative Pronouns

	PEOPLE		
SINGULAR	PLURAL		
que	que	who, that (subject)	(→1)
que	que	who(m), that (direct object)	(→2)
a quien	a quienes		
a quien	a quienes	to whom, that	(→3)
de que	de que	of whom, that	(→4)
de quien	de quienes		
cuyo/a	cuyos/as	whose	(→5)

	THINGS	
SINGULAR AND PLURAL		
que	which, that (subject)	(→6)
que	which, that (direct object)	(→7)
a que	to which, that	(→8)
de que	of which, that	(→9)
cuyo	whose	(→10)

But note that these forms can also refer to people

- **cuyo** agrees with the noun it accompanies, NOT WITH THE OWNER (→**5/10**)

- You cannot omit the relative pronoun in Spanish as you can in English (→**2/7**)

Continued

1 Mi hermano, que tiene veinte años, es el más joven
My brother, who is twenty, is the youngest

2 Los amigos que más quiero son …
The friends (that) I like best are …
María, a quien Daniel admira tanto, es …
Maria, whom Daniel admires so much, is …

3 Mis abogados, a quienes he escrito hace poco, están …
My lawyers, to whom I wrote recently, are …

4 La chica de que te hablé llega mañana
The girl (that) I told you about is coming tomorrow
los niños de quienes se ocupa Vd
the children (that) you look after

5 Vendrá la mujer cuyo hijo está enfermo
The woman whose son is ill will be coming

6 Hay una escalera que lleva a la buhardilla
There's a staircase which leads to the loft

7 La casa que hemos comprado tiene …
The house (which) we've bought has …
Este es el regalo que me ha mandado mi amiga
This is the present (that) my friend has sent to me

8 la tienda a que siempre va
the shop (which) she always goes to

9 las injusticias de que se quejan
the injustices (that) they're complaining about

10 la ventana cuyas cortinas están corridas
the window whose curtains are drawn

Relative Pronouns (contd)

el cual, el que

- These are used when the relative is separated from the word it refers to, or when it would otherwise be unclear which word it referred to. The pronouns always agree in number and gender with the noun (→**1**)
  El cual may also be used when the verb in the relative clause is separated from the relative pronoun (→**2**)

lo que, lo cual

- The neuter form **lo** is normally used when referring to an idea, statement or abstract noun. In certain expressions, the form **lo cual** may also be used as the subject of the relative clause (→**3**)

Relative pronouns after prepositions

- **Que** and **quienes** are generally used after the prepositions:

a	to (→**4**)
con	with (→**5**)
de	from, about, of (→**6**)
en	in, on, into (→**7**)

  It should be noted that **en que** can sometimes by translated by:
  - *where*. In this case it can also be replaced by **en donde** or **donde** (→**8**)
  - *when*. Sometimes here it can be replaced by **cuando** (→**9**)

- **El que** or **el cual** are used after other prepositions, and they always agree (→**10**)

Continued

1 **El padre de Elena, el cual tiene mucho dinero, es ...**
  Elena's father, who has a lot of money, is ...
  (**el cual** *is used here since* **que** *or* **quien** *might equally refer to Elena*)
  Su hermana, a la cual/la que hacía mucho que no veía, estaba también allí
  His sister, whom I hadn't seen for a long time, was also there

2 **Vieron a su tío, el cual, después de levantarse, salió**
  They saw their uncle, who, after having got up, went out

3 **No sabe lo que hace**
  He doesn't know what he is doing
  Lo que dijiste fue una tontería
  What you said was foolish
  Todo estaba en silencio, lo que (*or* **lo cual**) **me pareció muy raro**
  All was silent, which I thought most odd

4 **las tiendas a (las) que íbamos**
  the shops we used to go to

5 **la chica con quien** (*or* **la que**) **sale**
  the girl he's going out with

6 **el libro de(l) que te hablé**
  the book I told you about

7 **el lío en (el) que te has metido**
  the trouble you've got yourself into

8 **el sitio en que (en donde/donde) se escondía**
  the place where he/she was hiding

9 **el año en que naciste**
  the year (when) you were born

10 **el puente debajo del que/cual pasa el río**
  the bridge under which the river flows
  las obras por las cuales/que es famosa
  the plays for which she is famous

Relative Pronouns (contd)

el que, la que; los que, las que

These mean *the one(s) who/which, those who* (→**1**)
Note that **quien(es)** can replace **el que** etc when used in a general
sense (→**2**)

todos los que, todas las que

These mean *all who, all those/the ones which* (→**3**)

todo lo que

This translates *all that, everything that* (→**4**)

el de, la de; los de, las de

These can mean:
  — *the one(s) of, that/those of* (→**5**)
  — *the one(s) with* (→**6**)

1 Esa película es la que quiero ver
That film is the one I want to see
¿Te acuerdas de ese amigo? El que te presenté ayer
Do you remember that friend? The one I introduced you to
yesterday
Los que quieran entrar tendrán que pagar
Those who want to go in will have to pay

2 Quien (or el que) llegue antes ganará el premio
He who arrives first will win the prize

3 Todos los que salían iban de negro
All those who were coming out were dressed in black
**¿Qué autobuses puedo tomar? — Todos los que pasen por
aquí**
Which buses can I take? — Any (All those) that come this way

4 Quiero saber todo lo que ha pasado
I want to know all that has happened

5 Trae la foto de tu novio y la de tu hermano
Bring the photo of your boyfriend and the one of your brother
Viajamos en mi coche y en el de María
We travelled in my car and Maria's
Te doy estos libros y también los de mi hermana
I'll give you these books and my sister's too

6 Tu amigo, el de las gafas, me lo contó
Your friend, the one with glasses, told me

Interrogative Pronouns

¿qué?	*what?; which?*
¿cuál(es)?	*which?; what?*
¿quién(es)?	*who?*

qué

It always translates *what* (→**1**)
Note, however, that **por** + **qué** is normally translated by *why*
(→**2**)

cuál

It normally implies a choice, and translates *which* (→**3**) EXCEPT
when no choice is implied or more specific information is required
(→**4**)
Note that whilst the pronoun **qué** can also work as an adjective,
cuál only works as a pronoun (→**5**)

quién

—	**quién(es)** (subject or after preposition)	*who*	(→**6**)
—	**a quién(es)** (object)	*whom*	(→**7**)
—	**de quién(es)**	*whose*	(→**8**)

• All the forms shown above are also used in indirect questions
(→**9**)

1 **¿Qué estan haciendo?**
What are they doing?
¿Para qué lo quieres?
What do you want it for?

¿Qué dices?
What are you saying?

2 **¿Por qué no llegaron Vds antes?**
Why didn't you arrive earlier?

3 **¿Cuál de estos vestidos te gusta más?**
Which of these dresses do you like best?
¿Cuáles viste?
Which ones did you see?

4 **¿Cuál es la capital de España?**
What is the capital of Spain?
¿Cuál es tu consejo?
What is your advice?
¿Cuál es su fecha de nacimiento?
What is your date of birth?

5 **¿Qué libro es más interesante?**
Which book is more interesting?
¿Cuál (de estos libros) es más interesante?
Which (of these books) is more interesting?

6 **¿Quién ganó la carrera?**
Who won the race?
¿Con quiénes los viste?
Who did you see them with?

7 **¿A quiénes ayudaste?**
Who(m) did you help?

¿A quién se lo diste?
Who did you give it to?

8 **¿De quién es este libro?**
Whose is this book?

9 **Le pregunté para qué lo quería**
I asked him/her what he/she wanted it for
No me dijeron cuáles preferían
They didn't tell me which ones they preferred
No sabía a quién acudir
I didn't know who to turn to

Possessive Pronouns

These are the same as the strong forms of the possessive adjectives, but they are always accompanied by the definite article.

SINGULAR

MASCULINE	FEMININE	
el mío	la mía	*mine*
el tuyo	la tuya	*yours* (of **tú**)
el suyo	la suya	*his; hers; its; yours* (of **Vd**)
el nuestro	la nuestra	*ours*
el vuestro	la vuestra	*yours* (of **vosotros**)
el suyo	la suya	*theirs; yours* (of **Vds**)

PLURAL

MASCULINE	FEMININE	
los míos	las mías	*mine*
los tuyos	las tuyas	*yours* (of **tú**)
los suyos	las suyas	*his; hers; its; yours* (of **Vd**)
los nuestros	las nuestras	*ours*
los vuestros	las vuestras	*yours* (of **vosotros**)
los suyos	las suyas	*theirs; yours* (of **Vds**)

- The pronoun agrees in number and gender with the noun it replaces, NOT WITH THE OWNER (→1)

- Alternative translations are *my own, your own*, etc (→2)

- After the prepositions **a** and **de** the article **el** is contracted in the normal way (see p 196)

  a + el mío → al mío (→3)
  de + el mío → del mío (→4)

1 Pregunta a Cristina si este bolígrafo es el suyo
Ask Christine if this pen is hers
¿Qué equipo ha ganado, el suyo o el nuestro?
Which team won — theirs or ours?
Mi perro es más joven que el tuyo
My dog is younger than yours
Daniel pensó que esos libros eran los suyos
Daniel thought those books were his
Si no tienes discos, te prestaré los míos
If you don't have any records, I'll lend you mine
Las habitaciones son menos amplias que las vuestras
The rooms are smaller than yours

2 ¿Es su familia tan grande como la tuya?
Is his/her/their family as big as your own?
Sus precios son más bajos que los nuestros
Their prices are lower than our own

3 ¿Por qué prefieres este sombrero al mío?
Why do you prefer this hat to mine?
Su coche se parece al vuestro
His/her/their car looks like yours

4 Mi libro está encima del tuyo
My book is on top of yours
Su padre vive cerca del nuestro
His/her/their father lives near ours

Demonstrative Pronouns

	MASCULINE	FEMININE	NEUTER	
SING	éste	ésta	esto	this
	ése	ésa	eso	that
	aquél	aquélla	aquello	
PLUR	éstos	éstas		these
	ésos	ésas		those
	aquéllos	aquéllas		

- The pronoun agrees in number and gender with the noun it replaces (→1)

- The difference in meaning between the forms **ése** and **aquél** is the same as between the corresponding adjectives (see p 212)

- The masculine and feminine forms have an accent, which is the only thing that differentiates them from the corresponding adjectives.

- The neuter forms always refer to an idea or a statement or to an object when we want to identify it, etc, but never to specified nouns (→2)

- An additional meaning of **aquél** is *the former*, and of **éste** *the latter* (→3)

1 ¿Qué abrigo te gusta más? — Este de aquí
Which coat do you like best? — This one here
Aquella casa era más grande que ésta
That house was bigger than this one
estos libros y aquéllos
these books and those (over there)
Quiero estas sandalias y ésas
I'd like these sandals and those ones

2 No puedo creer que esto me esté pasando a mí
I can't believe this is really happening to me
Eso de madrugar es algo que no le gusta
(This business of) getting up early is something she doesn't like
Aquello sí que me gustó
I really did like that
Esto es una bicicleta
This is a bicycle

3 Hablaban Jaime y Andrés, éste a voces y aquél casi en un susurro
James and Andrew were talking, the latter in a loud voice and the former almost in a whisper

Adverbs

Formation

- Most adverbs are formed by adding **-mente** to the feminine form of the adjective. Accents on the adjective are not affected since the suffix **-mente** is stressed independently (**→1**)

  Note, however, that **-mente** is omitted:
  - In the first of two or more of these adverbs when joined by a conjunction (**→2**)
  - In **recientemente** *recently* when immediately preceding a past participle (**→3**). An accent is then needed on the last syllable (see p 292)

- The following adverbs are formed in an irregular way:

bueno	→	**bien**
good		*well*
malo	→	**mal**
bad		*badly*

Adjectives used as adverbs

Certain adjectives are used adverbially. These include:
alto, bajo, barato, caro, claro, derecho, fuerte and **rápido** (**→4**)
It should be noted that other adjectives used as adverbs agree with the subject, and can normally be replaced by the adverb ending in **-mente** or an adverbial phrase (**→5**)

Position of Adverbs

- When the adverb accompanies a verb, it may either immediately follow it or precede it for emphasis (**→6**)

  Note, however, that the adverb can never be placed between **haber** and the past participle in compound tenses (**→7**)

- When the adverb accompanies an adjective or another adverb, it generally precedes the adjective or adverb (**→8**)

Continued

1 *FEM ADJECTIVE*	*ADVERB*
lenta slow	**lentamente** slowly
franca frank	**francamente** frankly
feliz happy	**felizmente** happily
fácil easy	**fácilmente** easily

2 Lo hicieron lenta pero **eficazmente**
They did it slowly but efficiently

3 El pan estaba recién hecho
The bread had just been baked

4 hablar alto/bajo | **cortar derecho**
to speak loudly/softly | to cut (in a) straight (line)
costar barato/caro | **Habla muy fuerte**
to be cheap/expensive | He talks very loudly
ver claro | **correr rápido**
to see clearly | to run fast

5 Esperaban impacientes (*or* **impacientemente/con impaciencia**)
They were waiting impatiently
Vivieron muy felices (*or* **muy felizmente**)
They lived very happily

6 No conocemos aún al nuevo médico
We still haven't met the new doctor
Aún estoy esperando
I'm still waiting
Han hablado muy bien
They have spoken very well
Siempre le regalaban flores
They always gave her flowers

7 Lo he hecho ya
I've already done it
No ha estado nunca en Italia
She's never been to Italy

8 un sombrero muy bonito | **hablar demasiado alto**
a very nice hat | to talk too loud
mañana temprano | **hoy mismo**
early tomorrow | today

Comparatives and Superlatives

Comparatives

These are formed using the following constructions:

más ... (que)	more ... (than)	(→1)
menos ... (que)	less ... (than)	(→2)
tanto como	as much as	(→3)
tan ... como	as ... as	(→4)
tan ... que	so ... that	(→5)
demasiado ... para	too ... to	(→6)
(lo) bastante ... (lo) suficientemente ... } para	enough to	(→7)
cada vez más/menos	more and more/less and less	(→8)

Superlatives

- These are formed by placing **más/menos** *the most/the least* before the adverb (→9)

- **lo** is added before a superlative which is qualified (→10)

- The absolute superlative (*very, most, extremely* + adverb) is formed by placing **muy** before the adverb. The form **-ísimo** (see also p 292) is also occasionally found (→11)

Adverbs with irregular comparatives/superlatives

ADVERB	COMPARATIVE	SUPERLATIVE
bien	**mejor***	**(lo) mejor**
well	*better*	*(the) best*
mal	**peor**	**(lo) peor**
badly	*worse*	*(the) worst*
mucho	**más**	**(lo) más**
a lot	*more*	*(the) most*
poco	**menos**	**(lo) menos**
little	*less*	*(the) least*

***más bien** also exists, meaning *rather* (→12)

Continued

1 **más de prisa**   **más abiertamente**
   more quickly   more openly
   Mi hermana canta más fuerte que yo
   My sister sings louder than me

2 **menos fácilmente**   **menos a menudo**
   less easily   less often
   Nos vemos menos frecuentemente que antes
   We see each other less frequently than before

3 **Daniel no lee tanto como Andrés**
   Daniel doesn't read as much as Andrew

4 **Hágalo tan rápido como le sea posible**
   Do it as quickly as you can
   Ganan tan poco como nosotros
   They earn as little as we do

5 **Llegaron tan pronto que tuvieron que esperarnos**
   They arrived so early that they had to wait for us

6 **Es demasiado tarde para ir al cine**
   It's too late to go to the cinema

7 **Eres (lo) bastante grande para hacerlo solo**
   You're old enough to do it by yourself

8 **Me gusta el campo cada vez más**
   I like the countryside more and more

9 **María es la que corre más rápido**
   Maria is the one who runs fastest
   El que llegó menos tarde fue Miguel
   Miguel was the one to arrive the least late

10 **Lo hice lo más de prisa que pude**
   I did it as quickly as I could

11 **muy lentamente**   **tempranísimo**   **muchísimo**
   very slowly   extremely early   very much

12 **Era un hombre más bien bajito**
   He was a rather short man
   Estaba más bien inquieta que impaciente
   I was restless rather than impatient

Common Adverbs and their usage

bastante	enough; quite	(→1)
bien	well	(→2)
cómo	how	(→3)
cuánto	how much	(→4)
demasiado	too much; too	(→5)
más	more	(→6)
menos	less	(→7)
mucho	a lot; much	(→8)
poco	little, not much; not very	(→9)
siempre	always	(→10)
también	also, too	(→11)
tan	as	(→12)
tanto	as much	(→13)
todavía/aún	still; yet; even	(→14)
ya	already	(→15)

- **bastante, cuánto, demasiado, mucho, poco** and **tanto** are also used as adjectives that agree with the noun they qualify (see indefinite adjectives, p 220 and interrogative adjectives, p 214)

1 **Es bastante tarde**
   It's quite late
2 **¡Bien hecho!**
   Well done!
3 **¡Cómo me ha gustado!**
   How I liked it!
4 **¿Cuánto cuesta este libro?**
   How much is this book?
5 **He comido demasiado**   **Es demasiado caro**
   I've eaten too much   It's too expensive
6 **Mi hermano trabaja más ahora** **Es más tímida que Sofía**
   My brother works more now   She is shyer than Sophie
7 **Se debe beber menos**   **Estoy menos sorprendida que tú**
   One must drink less   I'm less surprised than you are
8 **¿Lees mucho?**   **¿Está mucho más lejos?**
   Do you read a lot?   Is it much further?
9 **Comen poco**   **María es poco decidida**
   They don't eat (very) much   Maria is not very daring
10 **Siempre dicen lo mismo**
   They always say the same (thing)
11 **A mí también me gusta**
   I like it too
12 **Ana es tan alta como yo**
   Ana is as tall as I am
13 **Nos aburrimos tanto como vosotros**
   We got as bored as you did
14 **Todavía/aún tengo dos**   **Todavía/aún no han llegado**
   I've still got two   They haven't arrived yet
   Mejor aún/todavía
   Even better
15 **Ya lo he hecho**
   I've done it already

On the following pages you will find some of the most frequent uses of prepositions in Spanish. Particular attention is paid to cases where usage differs markedly from English. It is often difficult to give an English equivalent for Spanish prepositions, since usage *does* vary so much between the two languages. In the list below, the broad meaning of the preposition is given on the left, with examples of usage following. Prepositions are dealt with in alphabetical order, except **a**, **de**, **en** and **por** which are shown first.

a

at	echar algo a algn	to throw sth at sb
	a 50 pesetas el kilo	(at) 50 pesetas a kilo
	a 100 km por hora	at 100 km per hour
	sentarse a la mesa	to sit down at the table
in	al sol	in the sun
	a la sombra	in the shade
onto	cayeron al suelo	they fell onto the floor
	pegar una foto al álbum	to stick a photo into the album
to	ir al cine	to go to the cinema
	dar algo a algn	to give sth to sb
	venir a hacer	to come to do
from	quitarle algo a algn	to take sth from sb
	robarle algo a algn	to steal sth from sb
	arrebatarle algo a algn	to snatch sth from sb
	comprarle algo a algn	to buy sth from/for sb*
	esconderle algo a algn	to hide sth from sb
means	a mano	by hand
	a caballo	on horseback (but note other forms of transport used with **en** and **por**)
	a pie	on foot

*The translation here obviously depends on the context

manner	**a la inglesa**	*in the English manner*
	a pasos lentos	*with slow steps*
	poco a poco	*little by little*
	a ciegas	*blindly*
time, date:	**a medianoche**	*at midnight*
at, on	**a las dos y cuarto**	*at quarter past two*
	a tiempo	*on time*
	a final/fines de mes	*at the end of the month*
	a veces	*at times*
distance	**a 8 km de aquí**	*(at a distance of) 8 kms from here*
	a dos pasos de mi casa	*just a step from my house*
	a lo lejos	*in the distance*
with **el** + infin	**al levantarse**	*on getting up*
	al abrir la puerta	*on opening the door*
after certain adjectives	**dispuesto a todo**	*ready for anything*
	parecido a esto	*similar to this*
	obligado a ello	*obliged to (do) that*
after certain verbs	see p 66	

Personal a

When the direct object of a verb is a person or pet animal, **a** must always be placed immediately before it.

EXAMPLES: **querían mucho a sus hijos**
                they loved their children dearly
                el niño miraba a su perro con asombro
                the boy kept looking at his dog in astonishment

EXCEPTION:	**tener**	**tienen dos hijos**
	to have	*they have two children*

Continued

de

from	**venir de Londres**	*to come from London*
	un médico de Valencia	*a doctor from Valencia*
	de la mañana a la noche	*from morning till night*
	de 10 a 15	*from 10 to 15*
belonging to, of	**el sombrero de mi padre**	*my father's hat*
	las lluvias de abril	*April showers*
contents, composition, material	**una caja de cerillas**	*a box of matches*
	una taza de té	*a cup of tea; a tea-cup*
	un vestido de seda	*a silk dress*
destined for	**una silla de cocina**	*a kitchen chair*
	un traje de noche	*an evening dress*
descriptive	**la mujer del sombrero verde**	*the woman with the green hat*
	el vecino de al lado	*the next door neighbour*
manner	**de manera irregular**	*in an irregular way*
	de una puñalada	*by stabbing*
quality	**una mujer de edad**	*an aged lady*
	objetos de valor	*valuable items*
comparative + number	**había más/menos de 100 personas**	*there were more/fewer than 100 people*
after superlatives: *in*	**la ciudad más/menos bonita del mundo**	*the most/least beautiful city in the world*
after certain adjectives	**contento de ver**	*pleased to see*
	fácil/difícil de entender	*easy/difficult to understand*
	capaz de hacer	*capable of doing*
after certain verbs	see p 66	

en

in, at	**en el campo**	*in the country*
	en Londres	*in London*
	en la cama	*in bed*
	con un libro en la mano	*with a book in his hand*
	en voz baja	*in a low voice*
	en la escuela	*in/at school*
into	**entra en la casa**	*go into the house*
	metió la mano en su bolso	*she put her hand into her handbag*
on	**un cuadro en la pared**	*a picture on the wall*
	sentado en una silla	*sitting on a chair*
	en la planta baja	*on the ground floor*
time, dates, months: *at, in*	**en este momento**	*at this moment*
	en 1994	*in 1994*
	en enero	*in January*
transport: *by*	**en coche**	*by car*
	en avión	*by plane*
	en tren	*by train (but see also por)*
language	**en español**	*in Spanish*
duration	**lo haré en una semana**	*I'll do it in one week*
after certain adjectives	**es muy buena/mala en geografía**	*she is very good/bad at geography*
	fueron los primeros/ últimos/únicos en + infin	*they were the first/ last/only ones + infin*
after certain verbs	see p 66	

Continued

por

motion: along, through, around	**vaya por ese camino** **por el túnel** **pasear por el campo**	*go along that path* *through the tunnel* *to walk around the countryside*
vague location	**tiene que estar por aquí** **le busqué por todas partes**	*it's got to be somewhere around here* *I looked for him everywhere*
vague time	**por la tarde** **por aquellos días**	*in the afternoon* *in those days*
rate	**90 km por hora** **un cinco por ciento** **ganaron por 3 a 0**	*90 km per hour* *five per cent* *they won by 3 to 0*
agent of passive: by	**descubierto por unos niños** **odiado por sus enemigos**	*discovered by some children* *hated by his enemies*
by (means of)	**por barco** **por tren** **por correo aéreo** **llamar por teléfono**	*by boat* *by train (freight)* *by airmail* *to telephone*
cause, reason: for, because	**¿por qué?** **por todo eso** **por lo que he oído**	*why?, for what reason?* *because of all that* *judging by what I've heard*
+ infinitive: to	**libros por leer** **cuentas por pagar**	*books to be read* *bills to be paid*
equivalence	**¿me tienes por tonto?**	*do you think I'm stupid?*
+ adjective/ adverb + que: however	**por buenos que sean** **por mucho que lo quieras**	*however good they are* *however much you want it*

por (contd)

for	¿cuanto me darán por este libro?	how much will they give me for this book?
	te lo cambio por éste	I'll swap you this one for it
	no siento nada por ti	I feel nothing for you
	si no fuera por ti	if it weren't for you
	¡Por Dios!	For God's sake!
for the benefit of	lo hago por ellos	I do it for their benefit
on behalf of	firma por mí	sign on my behalf

por also combines with other prepositions to form double prepositions usually conveying the idea of movement. The commonest of these are:

over	saltó por encima de la mesa	she jumped over the table
under	nadamos por debajo del puente	we swam under the bridge
past	pasaron por delante de Correos	they went past the Post Office
behind	por detrás de la puerta	behind the door
through	la luz entraba por entre las cortinas	light was coming in through the curtains
+ donde	¿por dónde has venido?	which way did you come?

ante

faced with, before	lo hicieron ante mis propios ojos	they did it before my very eyes
	ante eso no se puede hacer nada	one can't do anything when faced with that
preference	la salud ante todo	health above all things

antes de

before (time)	antes de las 5	before 5 o'clock

bajo/debajo de

These are usually equivalent, although **bajo** is used more frequently in a figurative sense and with temperatures.

under	**bajo/debajo de la cama**	*under the bed*
	bajo el dominio romano	*under Roman rule*
below	**un grado bajo cero**	*one degree below zero*

con

with	**vino con su amigo**	*she came with her friend*
after certain adjectives	**enfadado con ellos**	*angry with them*
	magnánimo con sus súbditos	*magnanimous with his subjects*

contra

against	**no tengo nada contra ti**	*I've nothing against you*
	apoyado contra la pared	*leaning against the wall*

delante de

in front of	**iba delante de mí**	*she was walking in front of me*

desde

from	**desde aquí se puede ver**	*you can see it from here*
	llamaban desde España	*they were phoning from Spain*
	desde otro punto de vista	*from a different point of view*
	desde la 1 hasta las 6	*from 1 till 6*
	desde entonces	*from then onwards*
since	**desde que volvieron**	*since they returned*
for	**viven en esa casa desde hace 3 años**	*they've been living in that house for 3 years* (NOTE TENSE)

detrás de

behind	**están detrás de la puerta**	they are behind the door

durante

during	**durante la guerra**	during the war
for	**anduvieron durante 3 días**	they walked for 3 days

entre

between	**entre 8 y 10**	between 8 and 10
among	**María y Elena, entre otras**	Maria and Elena, among others
reciprocal	**ayudarse entre sí**	to help each other

excepto

except (for)	**todos excepto tú**	everybody except you

hacia

towards	**van hacia ese edificio**	they're going towards that building
around (time)	**hacia las 3**	at around 3 (o'clock)
	hacia fines de enero	around the end of January

Hacia can also combine with some adverbs to convey a sense of motion in a particular direction:

hacia arriba	upwards
hacia abajo	downwards
hacia adelante	forwards
hacia atrás	backwards
hacia adentro	inwards
hacia afuera	outwards

Continued

hasta

until	**hasta la noche**	*until night*
as far as	**viajaron hasta Sevilla**	*they travelled as far as Seville*
up to	**conté hasta 300 ovejas**	*I counted up to 300 lambs*
	hasta ahora no los había visto	*up to now I hadn't seen them*
even	**hasta un tonto lo entendería**	*even an imbecile would understand that*

para

for	**es para ti**	*it's for you*
	es para mañana	*it's for tomorrow*
	una habitación para dos noches	*a room for two nights*
	para ser un niño, lo hace muy bien	*for a child he is very good at it*
	salen para Cádiz	*they are leaving for Cádiz*
	se conserva muy bien para sus años	*he keeps very well for his age*
+ infin:	**es demasiado torpe**	*he's too stupid to understand*
(in order) to	**para comprenderlo**	
+ sí:	**hablar para sí**	*to talk to oneself*
to oneself	**reír para sí**	*to laugh to oneself*
with time	**todavía tengo para 1 hora**	*I'll be another hour (at it) yet*

salvo

except (for)	**todos salvo él**	*all except him*
	salvo cuando llueve	*except when it's raining*
barring	**salvo imprevistos**	*barring the unexpected*
	salvo contraorden	*unless you hear to the contrary*

según

| according to | según su consejo | according to her advice |
| | según lo que me dijiste | according to what you told me |

sin

without	sin agua/dinero	without water/money
	sin mi marido	without my husband
+ infinitive	sin contar a los otros	without counting the others

sobre

on	sobre la cama	on the bed
	sobre el armario	on (top of) the wardrobe
on (to)	póngalo sobre la mesa	put it on the table
about, on	un libro sobre Eva Perón	a book about Eva Perón
above, over	volábamos sobre el mar	we were flying over the sea
	la nube sobre aquella montaña	the cloud above that mountain
approximately:	vendré sobre las 4	I'll come about 4 o'clock
about	Madrid tiene sobre 4 millones de habitantes	Madrid has about 4 million inhabitants

tras

behind	está tras el asiento	it's behind the seat
after	uno tras otro	one after another
	día tras día	day after day
	corrieron tras el ladrón	they ran after the thief

Conjunctions

There are conjunctions which introduce a main clause, such as **y** *and*, **pero** *but*, **si** *if*, **o** *or* etc, and those which introduce subordinate clauses like **porque** *because*, **mientras que** *while*, **después de que** *after* etc. They are used in much the same way as in English, but the following points are of note:

- Some conjunctions in Spanish require a following subjunctive, see pp 60 to 63

- Some conjunctions are 'split' in Spanish like *both ... and*, *either ... or* in English:

tanto ... como	*both ... and*	(→**1**)
ni ... ni	*neither ... nor*	(→**2**)
o (bien) ... o (bien)	*either ... or (else)*	(→**3**)
sea ... sea	*either ... or,*	(→**4**)
	whether ... or	

- **y**
  - Before words beginning with **i-** or **hi** + consonant it becomes **e** (→**5**)

- **o**
  - Before words beginning with **o-** or **ho-** it becomes **u** (→**6**)
  - Between numerals it becomes **ó** (→**7**)

- **que**
  - meaning *that* (→**8**)
  - in comparisons, meaning *than* (→**9**)
  - followed by the subjunctive, see p 58

- **porque** (Not to be confused with **por qué** *why*)
  - **como** should be used instead at the beginning of a sentence (→**10**)

- **pero, sino**
  - **pero** normally translates *but* (→**11**)
  - **sino** is used when there is a direct contrast after a negative (→**12**)

1 Estas flores crecen tanto en verano como en invierno
These flowers grow in both summer and winter

2 Ni él ni ella vinieron
Neither he nor she came
No tengo ni dinero ni comida
I have neither money nor food

3 Debe de ser o ingenua o tonta
She must be either naïve or stupid
O bien me huyen o bien no me reconocen
Either they're avoiding me or else they don't recognize me

4 Sea en verano, sea en invierno, siempre me gusta andar
I always like walking, whether in summer or in winter

5 Diana e Isabel
Diana and Isabel
madre e hija   *but*   **árboles y hierba**
mother and daughter   trees and grass

6 diez u once   **minutos u horas**
ten or eleven   minutes or hours

7 37 ó 38
37 or 38

8 Dicen que te han visto
They say (that) they've seen you
¿Sabías que estábamos allí?
Did you know that we were there?

9 Le gustan más que nunca
He likes them more than ever
María es menos guapa que su hermana
Maria is less attractive than her sister

10 Como estaba lloviendo no pudimos salir
Because/As it was raining we couldn't go out
(Compare with: **No pudimos salir porque estaba lloviendo**)

11 Me gustaría ir, pero estoy muy cansada
I'd like to go, but I am very tired

12 No es escocesa sino irlandesa
She is not Scottish but Irish

Augmentative, diminutive and pejorative suffixes

These can be used after nouns, adjectives and some adverbs. They are attached to the end of the word after any final vowel has been removed

e.g.   **puerta** → **puertita**
       doctor → **doctorcito**

Note however that further changes sometimes take place (see p 296)

Augmentatives

These are used mainly to imply largeness, but they can also suggest clumsiness, ugliness or grotesqueness. The commonest augmentatives are:

ón/ona	(→1)
azo/a	(→2)
ote/a	(→3)

Diminutives

These are used mainly to suggest smallness or to express a feeling of affection. Occasionally they can be used to express ridicule or contempt. The commonest diminutives are:

ito/a	(→4)
(e)cito/a	(→5)
(ec)illo/a	(→6)
(z)uelo/a	(→7)

Pejoratives

These are used to convey the idea that something is unpleasant or to express contempt. The commonest suffixes are:

ucho/a	(→8)
acho/a	(→9)
uzo/a	(→10)
uco/a	(→11)
astro/a	(→12)

ORIGINAL WORD	DERIVED FORM
1 **un hombre** a man	**un hombrón** a big man
2 **bueno** good	**buenazo** (person) easily imposed on
un perro a dog	**un perrazo** a really big dog
gripe flu	**un gripazo** a really bad bout of flu
3 **grande** big	**grandote** huge
palabra word	**palabrota** swear word
amigo friend	**amigote** old pal
4 **una casa** a house	**una casita** a cottage
un poco a little	**un poquito** a little bit
un rato a while	**un ratito** a little while
mi hija my daughter	**mi hijita** my dear sweet daughter
despacio slowly	**despacito** nice and slowly
5 **un viejo** an old man	**un viejecito** a little old man
un pueblo a village	**un pueblecito** a small village
una voz a voice	**una vocecita** a sweet little voice
6 **una ventana** a window	**una ventanilla** a small window (car, train etc)
un chico a boy	**un chiquillo** a small boy
una campana a bell	**una campanilla** a small bell
un palo a stick	**un palillo** a toothpick
un médico a doctor	**un mediquillo** a quack (doctor)
7 **los pollos** the chickens	**los polluelos** the little chicks
hoyos hollows	**hoyuelos** dimples
un ladrón a thief	**un ladronzuelo** a petty thief
una mujer a woman	**una mujerzuela** a whore
8 **un animal** an animal	**un animalucho** a wretched animal
un cuarto a room	**un cuartucho** a poky little room
una casa a house	**una casucha** a shack
9 **rico** rich	**ricacho** nouveau riche
10 **gente** people	**gentuza** scum
11 **una ventana** a window	**un ventanuco** a miserable little window
12 **un político** a politician	**un politicastro** a 3rd-rate politician

Word order

Word order in Spanish is much more flexible than in English. You can often find the subject placed after the verb or the object before the verb, either for emphasis or for stylistic reasons (→**1**)

There are some cases, however, where the order is always different from English. Most of these have already been dealt with under the appropriate part of speech, but are summarized here along with other instances not covered elsewhere.

- Object pronouns nearly always come before the verb (→**2**)
  For details, see pp 228 to 231

- Qualifying adjectives nearly always come after the noun (→**3**)
  For details, see p 224

- Following direct speech the subject always follows the verb (→**4**)

For word order in negative sentences, see p 272
For word order in interrogative sentences, see p 276

1 Ese libro te lo di yo
I gave you that book
No nos vio nadie
Nobody saw us

2 Ya los veo
I can see them now

Me lo dieron ayer
They gave it to me yesterday

3 una ciudad española
a Spanish town

vino tinto
red wine

4 — Pienso que sí — dijo María
'I think so,' said Maria
— No importa — replicó Daniel
'It doesn't matter,' Daniel replied

Negatives

A sentence is made negative by adding **no** between the subject and the verb (and any preceding object pronouns) (→**1**)
There are, however, some points to note:
— in phrases like *not her, not now,* etc the Spanish **no** usually comes after the word it qualifies (→**2**)
— with verbs of saying, hoping, thinking etc *not* is translated by **que no** (→**3**)

Double negatives

no ... nada	nothing	(not ... anything)
no ... nadie	nobody	(not ... anybody)
no ... más	no longer	(not ... any more)
no ... nunca	never	(not ... ever)
no ... jamás	never (stronger)	(not ... ever)
no ... más que	only	(not ... more than)
no ... ningún(o)(a)	no	(not any)
no ... tampoco	not ... either	
no ... ni ... ni	neither ... nor	
no ... ni siquiera	not even	

Word order

● **No** precedes the verb (and any object pronouns) in both simple and compound tenses, and the second element follows the verb (→**4**)

● Sometimes the above negatives are placed before the verb (with the exception of **más** and **más que**), and **no** is then dropped (→**5**)

● For use of **nada**, **nadie** and **ninguno** as pronouns, see p 236

Continued

1 AFFIRMATIVE   NEGATIVE

El coche es suyo   →   **El coche no es suyo**
The car is his   The car is not his

Yo me lo pondré   →   **Yo no me lo pondré**
I will put it on   I will not put it on

2 ¿Quién lo ha hecho? — Ella no
Who did it? — Not her

¿Quieres un cigarrillo? — Ahora no
Do you want a cigarette? — Not now

Dame ese libro, el que está a tu lado no, el otro
Give me that book, not the one near you, the other one

3 Opino que no   **Dijeron que no**
I think not   They said not

4 No dicen nada
They don't say anything

No han visto a nadie
They haven't seen anybody

No me veréis más
You won't see me any more

No te olvidaré nunca/jamás
I'll never forget you

No habían recorrido más que 40 kms cuando ...
They hadn't travelled more than 40 kms when ...

No se me ha ocurrido ninguna idea
I haven't had any ideas

No les estaban esperando ni mi hijo ni mi hija
Neither my son nor my daughter were waiting for them

No ha venido ni siquiera Juan
Even John hasn't come

5 Nadie ha venido hoy
Nobody came today

Nunca me han gustado
I've never liked them

Ni mi hermano ni mi hermana fuman
Neither my brother nor my sister smokes

Negatives (contd)

Negatives in short replies

- **No**, *no* is the usual negative response to a question (→**1**)
  Note, however, that it is often translated as *not* (→**2**) (see also p 272)

- Nearly all the other negatives listed on p 272 may be used without a verb in a short reply (→**3**)

Combinations of negatives

These are the most common combinations of negative particles:

no ... nunca más	(→**4**)
no ... nunca a nadie	(→**5**)
no ... nunca nada/nada nunca	(→**6**)
no ... nunca más que	(→**7**)
no ... ni ... nunca	(→**8**)

1 ¿Quieres venir con nosotros? — No
Do you want to come with us? — No

2 ¿Vienes o no?
Are you coming or not?

3 ¿Ha venido alguien? — ¡Nadie!
Has anyone come? — Nobody!
¿Has ido al Japón alguna vez? — Nunca
Have you ever been to Japan? — Never

4 No lo haré nunca más
I'll never do it again

5 No se ve nunca a nadie por allí
You never see anybody around there

6 No cambiaron nada nunca
They never changed anything

7 No he hablado nunca más que con su mujer
I've only ever spoken to his wife

8 No me ha escrito ni llamado por teléfono nunca
He/she has never written to me or phoned me

Question forms

Direct

There are two ways of forming direct questions in Spanish:

- by inverting the normal word order so that
  subject + verb → verb + subject (→**1**)

- by maintaining the word order *subject + verb*, but by using a
  rising intonation at the end of the sentence (→**2**)

It should be noted that in compound tenses the auxiliary may
never be separated from the past participle, as happens in English
(→**3**)

Indirect

An indirect question is one that is 'reported', e.g. he asked me
what the time was, tell me *which way to go*. Word order in
indirect questions can adopt one of the two following patterns:

- interrogative word + subject + verb (→**4**)

- interrogative word + verb + subject (→**5**)

¿verdad?, ¿no?

These are used wherever English would use *isn't it?, don't they?,
weren't we?, is it?* etc tagged on to the end of a sentence (→**6**)

sí

Sí is the word for yes in answer to a question put either in the
affirmative or in the negative (→**7**)

1 **¿Vendrá tu madre?**   **¿Lo trajo Vd?**
Will your mother come?   Did you bring it?
¿Es posible eso?   **¿Cuándo volverán Vds?**
Is it possible?   When will you come back?

2 **El gato, ¿se bebió toda la leche?**
Did the cat drink up all his milk?
Andrés, ¿va a venir?
Is Andrew coming?

3 **¿Lo ha terminado Vd?**   **¿Había llegado tu amigo?**
Have you finished it?   Had your friend arrived?

4 **Dime qué autobuses pasan por aquí**
Tell me which buses come this way
No sé cuántas personas vendrán
I don't know how many people will turn up

5 **Me preguntó dónde trabajaba mi hermano**
He asked me where my brother worked
No sabemos a qué hora empieza la película
We don't know what time the film starts

6 **Hace calor, ¿verdad?**
It's warm, isn't it?
No se olvidará Vd, ¿verdad?
You won't forget, will you?
Estaréis cansados, ¿no?
You will be tired, won't you?
Te lo dijo María, ¿no?
Maria told you, didn't she?

7 **¿Lo has hecho? — Sí**
Have you done it? — Yes (I have)
¿No lo has hecho? — Sí
Haven't you done it? — Yes (I have)

Beware of translating word by word. While on occasions this is quite possible, quite often it is not. The need for caution is illustrated by the following:

- English phrasal verbs (i.e. verbs followed by a preposition) e.g. *to run away, to fall down* are often translated by one word in Spanish (→**1**)

- English verbal constructions often contain a preposition where none exists in Spanish, or vice versa (→**2**)

- Two or more prepositions in English may have a single rendering in Spanish (→**3**)

- A word which is singular in English may be plural in Spanish, or vice versa (→**4**)

- Spanish has no equivalent of the possessive construction denoted by ...'s/...s' (→**5**)

Specific problems
-ing

This is translated in a variety of ways in Spanish:

- *to be ... -ing* can sometimes be translated by a simple tense (see also pp 54 to 56) (→**6**)
  But, when a physical position is denoted, a past participle is used (→**7**)

- in the construction *to see/hear sb ... -ing*, use an infinitive (→**8**)

  -ing can also be translated by:
  — an infinitive (→**9**)
    (see p 46)
  — a perfect infinitive (→**10**)
    (see p 50)
  — a gerund (→**11**)
    (see p 52)
  — a noun (→**12**)

Continued

1 huir
to run away

caerse
to fall down

ceder
to give in

2 pagar
to pay for

mirar
to look at

escuchar
to listen to

encontrarse con
to meet

fijarse en
to notice

servirse de
to use

3 extrañarse de
to be surprised at

harto de
fed up with

soñar con
to dream of

contar con
to count on

4 unas vacaciones
a holiday

sus cabellos
his/her hair

la gente
people

mi pantalón
my trousers

5 el coche de mi hermano
my brother's car
(literally: ... of my brother)

el cuarto de las niñas
the children's bedroom
(literally: ... of the children)

6 Se va mañana
He/she is leaving tomorrow

¿Qué haces?
What are you doing?

7 Está sentado ahí
He is sitting over there

Estaba tendida en el suelo
She was lying on the ground

8 Les veo venir
I can see them coming

La he oído cantar
I've heard her singing

9 Me gusta ir al cine
I like going to the cinema

¡Deja de hablar!
Stop talking!

En vez de contestar
Instead of answering

Antes de salir
Before leaving

10 Después de haber abierto la caja, María ...
After opening the box, Maria ...

11 Pasamos la tarde fumando y charlando
We spent the afternoon smoking and chatting

12 El esquí me mantiene en forma
Skiing keeps me fit

to be
(See also Verbal Idioms, pp 74 to 76)

- In set expressions, describing physical and emotional conditions, **tener** is used:

tener calor/frío	to be warm/cold
tener hambre/sed	to be hungry/thirsty
tener miedo	to be afraid
tener razón	to be right

- Describing the weather, e.g. *what's the weather like?, it's windy/sunny,* use **hacer** (→**1**)

- For ages, e.g. *he is 6,* use **tener** (see also p 306) (→**2**)

there is/there are

- Both are translated by **hay** (→**3**)

can, be able

- Physical ability is expressed by **poder** (→**4**)

- If the meaning is *to know how to,* use **saber** (→**5**)

- *Can* + a 'verb of hearing or seeing etc' in English is not translated in Spanish (→**6**)

to

- Generally translated by **a** (→**7**)

- In time expressions, e.g. *10 to 6,* use **menos** (→**8**)

- When the meaning is *in order to,* use **para** (→**9**)

- Following a verb, as in *to try to do, to like to do,* see pp 46 and 48

- *easy/difficult/impossible* etc *to do* are translated by **fácil/difícil/imposible** etc **de hacer** (→**10**)

1 ¿Qué tiempo hace?
What's the weather like?

Hace bueno/malo/viento
It's lovely/miserable/windy

2 ¿Cuántos años tienes?
How old are you?

Tengo quince (años)
I'm fifteen

3 Hay un señor en la puerta
There's a gentleman at the door
Hay cinco libros en la mesa
There are five books on the table

4 No puedo salir contigo
I can't go out with you

5 ¿Sabes nadar?
Can you swim?

6 No veo nada
I can't see anything

¿Es que no me oyes?
Can't you hear me?

7 Dale el libro a Isabel
Give the book to Isabel

8 las diez menos cinco
five to ten

a las siete menos cuarto
at a quarter to seven

9 Lo hice para ayudaros
I did it to help you
Se inclinó para atarse el cordón de zapato
He bent down to tie his shoe-lace

10 Este libro es fácil/difícil de leer
This book is easy/difficult to read

282 TRANSLATION PROBLEMS

must

- When *must* expresses an assumption, **deber de** is often used (→**1**)

  Note, however, that this meaning is also often expressed by **deber** directly followed by the infinitive (→**2**)

- When it expresses obligation, there are three possible translations:
  - **tener que**   (→**3**)
  - **deber**   (→**4**)
  - **hay que** (impersonal) (→**5**)

may

- If *may* expresses possibility, it can be translated by:
  - **poder**
  - **puede (ser) que** + subjunctive } (→**6**)

- To express permission, use **poder** (→**7**)

will

- If *will* expresses willingness or desire rather than the future, the present tense of **querer** is used (→**8**)

would

- If *would* expresses willingness, use the preterite or imperfect of **querer** (→**9**)

- When a repeated or habitual action in the past is referred to, use
  - the imperfect (→**10**)
  - the imperfect of **soler** + infinitive (→**11**)

1 Ha debido de mentir
He must have lied
Debe de gustarle
She must like it

2 Debe estar por aquí cerca
It must be near here
Debo haberlo dejado en el tren
I must have left it on the train

3 Tenemos que salir temprano mañana
We must leave early tomorrow
Tengo que irme
I must go

4 Debo visitarles
I must visit them
Debéis escuchar lo que se os dice
You must listen to what is said to you

5 Hay que entrar por ese lado
One (We etc) must get in that way

6 Todavía puede cambiar de opinión
He may still change his mind
Creo que puede llover esta tarde
I think it may rain this afternoon
Puede (ser) que no lo sepa
She may not know

7 ¿Puedo irme?   Puede sentarse
May I go?   You may sit down

8 ¿Quiere Vd esperar un momento, por favor?
Will you wait a moment, please?
No quiere ayudarme
He won't help me

9 No quisieron venir
They wouldn't come

10 Las miraba hora tras hora
She would watch them for hours on end

11 Últimamente solía comer muy poco
Latterly he would eat very little

Pronunciation of Vowels

Spanish vowels are always clearly pronounced and not relaxed in unstressed syllables as happens in English.

	EXAMPLES	HINTS ON PRONUNCIATION
[a]	casa	Between English *a* as in *hat* and *u* as in *hut*
[e]	pensar	Similar to English *e* in *pet*
[i]	filo	Between English *i* as in *pin* and *ee* as in *been*
[o]	loco	Similar to English *o* in *hot*
[u]	luna	Between English *ew* as in *few* and *u* as in *put*

Pronunciation of Diphthongs

All these diphthongs are shorter than similar English diphthongs.

[ai]	baile, hay	Like *i* in *side*
[au]	causa	Like *ou* in *sound*
[ei]	peine, rey	Like *ey* in *grey*
[eu]	deuda	Like the vowel sounds in English *may you*, but without the sound of the *y*
[oi]	boina, voy	Like *oy* in *boy*

Semi-consonants

[j]	hacia, ya tiene, yeso labio, yo	*i* following a consonant and preceding a vowel, and *y* preceding a vowel are pronounced as *y* in English *yet*
[w]	agua, bueno arduo, ruido	*u* following a consonant and preceding a vowel is pronounced as *w* in English *walk* EXCEPTIONS: **gue, gui** (see p 286)

Pronunciation of Consonants

Some consonants are pronounced almost exactly as in English:
[l, m, n, f, k, and in some cases g]
Others, listed below, are similar to English, but differences should
be noted.

EXAMPLES

[p]	**p**adre	} They are not aspirated, unlike
[k]	**c**o**c**o	English *p*ot, *c*ook and *t*en.
[t]	**t**an	

[t]	**t**odo, **t**ú	} Pronounced with the tip of the
[d]	**d**oy, bal**d**e	tongue touching the upper front teeth and not the roof of the mouth as in English.

The following consonants are not heard in English:

EXAMPLES

[ß]	la**b**io	This is pronounced between upper and lower lips, which do not touch, unlike English *b* as in *b*end.
[ɣ]	ha**g**a	Similar to English *g* as in *g*ate, but tongue does not touch the soft palate.
[ɲ]	a**ñ**o	Similar to *ni* in o*ni*on
[x]	**j**ota	Like the guttural *ch* in lo*ch*.
[r]	pe**r**a	A single trill with the tip of the tongue against the teeth ridge.
[rr]	**r**ojo, pe**rr**o	A multiple trill with the tip of the tongue against the teeth ridge.

From spelling to sounds

Note the pronunciation of the following (groups of) letters.

LETTER	PRONOUNCED	
b,v	[b]	These letters have the same value. At the start of a breath group, and after written **m** and **n**, the sound is similar to English *boy* (→**1**)
	[β]	In all other positions, the sound is unknown in English (see p 285) (→**2**)
c	[k]	Before **a, o, u** or a consonant, like English *keep*, but not aspirated (→**3**)
	[θ/s]	Before **e, i** like English *thin*, or, in Latin America and parts of Spain, like English *same* (→**4**)
ch	[tʃ]	Like English *church* (→**5**)
d	[d]	At the start of the breath group and after **l** or **n**, it is pronounced similar to English *deep* (see p 285) (→**6**)
	[ð]	Between vowels and after consonants (except **l** or **n**), it is pronounced very like English *though* (→**7**)
	[(ð)]	At the end of words, and in the verb ending **-ado**, it is often not pronounced (→**8**)
g	[x]	Before **e, i**, pronounced gutturally, similar to English *loch* (→**9**)
	[g]	At the start of the breath group and after **n**, it is pronounced like English *get* (→**10**)
	[ɣ]	In other positions the sound is unknown in English (→**11**)
gue	[ge/ɣe]	The **u** is silent (→**12**)
gui	[gi/ɣi]	
güe	[gwe/ɣwe]	The **u** is pronounced like English *walk* (→**13**)
güi	[gwi/ɣwi]	

1	**bomba** ['bomba]	**voy** [boi]	**vicio** ['biθjo]
2	**hubo** ['uβo]	**de veras** [de 'βeras]	**lavar** [la'βar]
3	**casa** ['kasa]	**coco** ['koko]	**cumbre** ['kumbre]
4	**cero** ['θero/'sero]	**cinco** ['θiŋko/'siŋko]	
5	**mucho** ['mutʃo]	**chuchería** [tʃutʃe'ria]	
6	**doy** [doi]	**balde** ['balde]	**bondad** [bon'dað]
7	**modo** ['moðo]	**ideal** [iðe'al]	
8	**Madrid** [ma'ðri(ð)]	**comprado** [kom'pra(ð)o]	
9	**gente** ['xente]	**giro** ['xiro]	**general** [xene'ral]
10	**ganar** [ga'nar]	**pongo** ['poŋgo]	
11	**agua** ['aɣwa]	**agrícola** [a'ɣrikola]	
12	**guija** ['gixa]	**guerra** ['gerra]	**pague** ['paɣe]
13	**agüero** [a'ɣwero]	**argüir** [ar'ɣwir]	

From spelling to sounds (contd)

h	[-]	This is always silent (→**1**)
j	[x]	Like the guttural sound in English lo*ch*, but often aspirated at the end of a word (→**2**)
ll	[ʎ]	Similar to English *-ll-* in mi*ll*ion (→**3**)
	[j/ʒ]	In some parts of Spain and in Latin America, like English *yet* or plea*s*ure (→**4**)
-nv-	[mb]	This combination of letters is pronounced as in English *imb*ibe (→**5**)
ñ	[ɲ]	As in English o*ni*on (→**6**)
q	[k]	Always followed by silent letter **u**, and pronounced as in English *k*eep, but not aspirated (→**7**)
s	[s]	Except where mentioned below, like English *s*ing (→**8**)
	[z]	When followed by **b, d, g, l, m, n** like English *z*oo (→**9**)
w	[w]	Like English *v, w* (→**10**)
x	[ks]	Between vowels, often like English e*x*it (→**11**)
	[s]	Before a consonant, and, increasingly, even between vowels, like English *s*end (→**12**)
y	[j]	Like English *y*es (→**13**)
	[ʒ]	In some parts of Latin America, like English lei*s*ure (→**14**)
z	[θ]	Like English *th*in (→**15**)
	[s]	In some parts of Spain and in Latin America, like English *s*end (→**16**)

1	**hombre** ['ombre]	**hoja** ['oxa]	**ahorrar** [ao'rrar]
2	**jota** ['xota]	**tejer** [te'xer]	**reloj** [re'lo(h)]
3	**calle** ['kaʎe]	**llamar** [ʎa'mar]	
4	**pillar** [pi'jar/pi'ʒar]	**olla** ['oja/'oʒa]	
5	**enviar** [em'bjar]	**sin valor** ['sim ba'lor]	
6	**uña** ['uɲa]	**bañar** [ba'ɲar]	
7	**aquel** [a'kel]	**querer** [ke'rer]	
8	**está** [es'ta]	**serio** ['serjo]	
9	**desde** ['dezðe]	**mismo** ['mizmo]	**asno** ['azno]
10	**wáter** ['bater]	**Walkman** ® [wak'man]	
11	**éxito** ['eksito]	**máximo** ['maksimo]	
12	**extra** ['estra]	**sexto** ['sesto]	
13	**yo** [jo]	**yedra** ['jeðra]	
14	**yeso** ['ʒeso]	**yerno** ['ʒerno]	
15	**zapato** [θa'pato]	**zona** ['θona]	**luz** [luθ]
16	**zaguán** [sa'ɣwan]	**zueco** ['sweko]	**pez** [pes]

Normal Word Stress

There are simple rules to establish which syllable in a Spanish word is stressed. When an exception to these rules occurs an acute accent (stress-mark) is needed (see p 292). These rules are as follows:

— words ending in a vowel or combination of vowels, or with the consonants **-s** or **-n** are stressed on the next to last syllable. The great majority of Spanish words fall into this category (→**1**)

— words ending in a consonant other than **-s** or **-n** bear the stress on the last syllable (→**2**)

— a minority of words bear the stress on the second to last syllable, and these always need an accent (→**3**)

— some nouns change their stress from singular to plural (→**4**)

Stress in diphthongs

In the case of diphthongs there are rules to establish which of the vowels is stressed (see p 284 for pronunciation). These rules are as follows:

— diphthongs formed by the combination of a 'weak' vowel (**i**, **u**) and a 'strong' vowel (**a**, **e** or **o**) bear the stress on the strong vowel (→**5**)

— diphthongs formed by the combination of two 'weak' vowels bear the stress on the second vowel (→**6**)

But note that two 'strong' vowels don't form a diphthong but are pronounced as two separate vowels. In these cases stress follows the normal rules (→**7**)

1 casa
house

casas
houses

corre
he runs

corren
they run

palabra
word

palabras
words

crisis
crisis

crisis
crises

2 reloj
watch

verdad
truth

batidor
beater

3 murciélago
bat

pájaro
bird

4 carácter
character

caracteres
characters

régimen
regime

regímenes
regimes

5 baile
dance

boina
beret

peine
comb

causa
cause

reina
queen

6 fui
I went

viudo
widower

7 me mareo
I feel dizzy

caer
to fall

caos
chaos

correa
leash

The acute accent (´)

This is used in writing to show that a word is stressed contrary to the normal rules for stress (see p 290) (→**1**)

The following points should be noted:

- The same syllable is stressed in the plural form of adjectives and nouns as in the singular. To show this, it is necessary to
  - add an accent in the case of unaccented nouns and adjectives ending in **-n** (→**2**)
  - drop the accent from nouns and adjectives ending in **-n** or **-s** which have an accent on the last syllable (→**3**)

- The feminine form of accented nouns or adjectives does not have an accent (→**4**)

- When object pronouns are added to certain verb forms an accent is required to show that the syllable stressed in the verb form does not change. These verb forms are:
  - the gerund (→**5**)
  - the infinitive, when followed by two pronouns (→**6**)
  - imperative forms, except for the 2nd person plural (→**7**)

- The absolute superlative forms of adjectives are always accented (→**8**)

- Accents on adjectives are not affected by the addition of the adverbial suffix **-mente** (→**9**)

1 autobús		**revolución**
bus		revolution
relámpago		**árboles**
lightning		trees
2 orden	→	**órdenes**
order		orders
examen	→	**exámenes**
examination		examinations
joven	→	**jóvenes**
young		young
3 revolución	→	**revoluciones**
revolution		revolutions
autobús	→	**autobuses**
bus		buses
parlanchín	→	**parlanchines**
chatty		chatty
4 marqués	→	**marquesa**
marquis		marchioness
francés	→	**francesa**
French *(masc)*		French *(fem)*
5 comprando	→	**comprándo(se)lo**
buying		buying it (for him/her/them)
6 vender	→	**vendérselas**
to sell		to sell them to him/her/them
7 compra	→	**cómpralo**
buy		buy it
hagan	→	**háganselo**
do		do it for him/her/them
8 viejo	→	**viejísimo**
old		ancient
caro	→	**carísimo**
expensive		very expensive
9 fácil	→	**fácilmente**
easy		easily

The acute accent (contd)

It is also used to distinguish between the written forms of words which are pronounced the same but have a different meaning or function. These are as follows:

- Possessive adjectives/personal pronouns (→**1**)

- Demonstrative adjectives/demonstrative pronouns (→**2**)

- Interrogative and exclamatory forms of adverbs, pronouns and adjectives (→**3**)

  Note that the accent is used in indirect as well as direct questions and exclamations (→**4**)

- The pronoun **él** and the article **el** (→**5**)

- A small group of words which could otherwise be confused. These are:

de	of, from	**dé**	give (pres subj)	
mas	but	**más**	more	
si	if	**sí**	yes; himself etc	(→**6**)
solo/a	alone	**sólo**	only	(→**7**)
te	you	**té**	tea	

The dieresis (¨)

This is used only in the combinations **güi** or **güe** to show that the **u** is pronounced as a semi-consonant (see p 284) (→**8**)

1 **Han robado mi coche**
They've stolen my car
¿Te gusta tu trabajo?
Do you like your job?

A mí no me vio
He didn't see me
Tú, ¿que opinas?
What do you think?

2 **Me gusta esta casa**
I like this house
¿Ves aquellos edificios?
Can you see those buildings?

Me quedo con ésta
I'll take this one
Aquéllos son más bonitos
Those are prettier

3 **El chico con quien viajé**
The boy I travelled with
Donde quieras
Wherever you want

¿Con quién viajaste?
Who did you travel with?
¿Dónde encontraste eso?
Where did you find that?

4 **¿Cómo se abre?**
How does it open?

No sé cómo se abre
I don't know how it opens

5 **El puerto queda cerca**
The harbour's nearby

Él no quiso hacerlo
HE refused to do it

6 **si no viene**
if he doesn't come

Sí que lo sabe
Yes he DOES know

7 **Vino solo**
He came by himself

Sólo lo sabe él
Only he knows

8 **¡Qué vergüenza!**
How shocking!
En seguida averigüé dónde estaba
I found out straight away where it was

Regular spelling changes

The consonants **c**, **g** and **z** are modified by the addition of certain verb or plural endings and by some suffixes. Most of the cases where this occurs have already been dealt with under the appropriate part of speech, but are summarized here along with other instances not covered elsewhere.

Verbs

The changes set out below occur so that the consonant of the verb stem is always pronounced the same as in the infinitive. For verbs affected by these changes see the list of verbs on p 81.

INFINITIVE	CHANGE	TENSES AFFECTED
-car	c + e → -que	Present subj, pret (→1)
-cer, -cir	c + a, o → -za, -zo	Present, pres subj (→2)
-gar	g + e, i → -gue	Present subj, pret (→3)
-guar	gu + e → -güe	Present subj, pret (→4)
-ger, -gir	g + a, o → -ja, -jo	Present, pres subj (→5)
-guir	gu + a, o → -ga, -go	Present, pres subj (→6)
-zar	z + e → -ce	Present subj, pret (→7)

Noun and adjective plurals

SINGULAR	PLURAL
vowel + **z**	→ -ces (→8)

Nouns and adjectives + suffixes

ENDING	SUFFIX	NEW ENDING
vowel + **z** +	-cito	-cecito (→9)
-go, -ga +	-ito, -illo	-guito/a, -guillo/a (→10)
-co, -ca +	-ito, -illo	-quito/a, -quillo/a (→11)

Adjective absolute superlatives

ENDING	SUPERLATIVE
-co	-quísimo (→12)
-go	-guísimo (→13)
vowel + **z**	-císimo (→14)

1 Es inútil que lo busques aquí
It's no good looking for it here
Saqué dos entradas
I got two tickets
2 Hace falta que venzas tu miedo
You must overcome your fear
3 No creo que lleguemos antes
I don't think we'll be there any sooner
Ya le pagué
I've already paid her
4 Averigüé dónde estaba la casa
I found out where the house was
5 Cojo el autobús, es más barato
I take the bus, it's cheaper
6 ¿Sigo?
Shall I go on?
7 No permiten que se cruce la frontera
They don't allow people to cross the border
Nunca simpaticé mucho con él
I never got on very well with him

8 voz → voces			**luz → luces**	
voice voices			light lights	
veloz → veloces			**capaz → capaces**	
quick			capable	
9 luz	→		**lucecita**	
light			little light	
10 amigo	→		**amiguito**	
friend			chum	
11 chico	→		**chiquillo**	
boy			little boy	
12 rico	→		**riquísimo**	
rich			extremely rich	
13 largo	→		**larguísimo**	
long			very, very long	
14 feroz	→		**ferocísimo**	
fierce			extremely fierce	

A, a	[a]	**J, j**	['xota]	**R, r**	['erre]
B, b	[be]	**K, k**	[ka]	**S, s**	['ese]
C, c	[θe]	**L, l**	['ele]	**T, t**	[te]
D, d	[de]	**M, m**	['eme]	**U, u**	[u]
E, e	[e]	**N, n**	['ene]	**V, v**	['uβe]
F, f	['efe]	**Ñ, ñ**	['eɲe]	**W, w**	['uβe'doble]
G, g	[xe]	**O, o**	[o]	**X, x**	['ekis]
H, h	['atʃe]	**P, p**	[pe]	**Y, y**	[i'ɣrjeɣa]
I, i	[i]	**Q, q**	[ku]	**Z, z**	['θeta]

- **Ch** and **ll** no longer constitute separate letters in the Spanish alphabet. Words beginning with **ch** and **ll** are included under **C** and **L**.

- The letters are feminine and you therefore talk of **una a**, or **la a**

- Capital letters are used as in English except for the following:
  - adjectives of nationality:

e.g. **una ciudad alemana**   **un autor español**
    a German town   a Spanish author

  - languages:

e.g. **¿Habla Vd inglés?**   **Hablan español e italiano**
    Do you speak English?   They speak Spanish and
                                Italian

  - days of the week:

lunes	Monday	**viernes**	Friday
martes	Tuesday	**sábado**	Saturday
miércoles	Wednesday	**domingo**	Sunday
jueves	Thursday		

  - months of the year:

enero	January	**julio**	July
febrero	February	**agosto**	August
marzo	March	**se(p)tiembre**	September
abril	April	**octubre**	October
mayo	May	**noviembre**	November
junio	June	**diciembre**	December

Spanish punctuation differs from English in the following ways:

Question marks

There are inverted question marks and exclamation marks at the beginning of a question or exclamation, as well as upright ones at the end

Indications of dialogue

Dashes are used to indicate dialogue, and are equivalent to the English inverted commas:

— ¿Vendrás conmigo? — le preguntó María
'Will you come with me?' Maria asked him
Note, however, that when no expression of saying, replying etc follows, only one dash is used at the beginning:

— Sí. 'Yes.'

Letter headings

At the beginning of a letter, a colon is used instead of the English comma:

Querida Cristina: Dear Cristina, **Muy Sr. mío:** Dear Sir,

Punctuation terms in Spanish

.	punto	!	se cierra admiración
,	coma	" "	comillas (used as '...')
;	punto y coma	"	se abren comillas
:	dos puntos	"	se cierran comillas
...	puntos suspensivos	( )	paréntesis
¿ ?	interrogación	(	se abre paréntesis
¿	se abre interrogación	)	se cierra paréntesis
?	se cierra interrogación	—	guión
¡ !	admiración		
¡	se abre admiración	punto y aparte	new paragraph
		punto final	last full stop

Cardinal numbers *(one, two, three etc)*

cero	0	setenta	70
uno (un, una)	1	ochenta	80
dos	2	noventa	90
tres	3	cien (ciento)	100
cuatro	4	ciento uno(una)	101
cinco	5	ciento dos	102
seis	6	ciento diez	110
siete	7	ciento cuarenta y dos	142
ocho	8	doscientos(as)	200
nueve	9	doscientos(as) uno(una)	201
diez	10	doscientos(as) dos	202
once	11	trescientos(as)	300
doce	12	cuatrocientos(as)	400
trece	13	quinientos(as)	500
catorce	14	seiscientos(as)	600
quince	15	setecientos(as)	700
dieciséis	16	ochocientos(as)	800
diecisiete	17	novecientos(as)	900
dieciocho	18	mil	1.000
diecinueve	19	mil uno(una)	1.001
veinte	20	mil dos	1.002
veintiuno	21	mil doscientos veinte	1.220
veintidós	22	dos mil	2.000
treinta	30	cien mil	100.000
treinta y uno	31	doscientos(as) mil	200.000
cuarenta	40	un millón	1.000.000
cincuenta	50	dos millones	2.000.000
sesenta	60	un billón	1.000.000.000.000

Fractions

un medio; medio(a)	$\frac{1}{2}$
un tercio	$\frac{1}{3}$
dos tercios	$\frac{2}{3}$
un cuarto	$\frac{1}{4}$
tres cuartos	$\frac{3}{4}$
un quinto	$\frac{1}{5}$
cinco y tres cuartos	$5\frac{3}{4}$

Others

cero coma cinco	0,5
uno coma tres	1,3
(el, un) diez por ciento	10%
dos más/y dos	2 + 2
dos menos dos	2 − 2
dos por dos	2 × 2
dos dividido por dos	2 ÷ 2

Points to note on cardinals

- **uno** drops the **o** before masculine nouns, and the same applies when in compound numerals:
  un libro *1 book*, **treinta y un niños** *31 children*

- 1, 21, 31 etc and 200, 300, 400 etc have feminine forms:
  cuarenta y una pesetas *41 pesetas*, **quinientas libras** *£500*

- **ciento** is used before numbers smaller than 100, otherwise **cien** is used:
  ciento cuatro *104 but* **cien pesetas** *100 pesetas*, **cien mil** *100,000* (see also p 206)

- **millón** takes **de** before a noun:
  un millón de personas *1,000,000 people*

- **mil** is only found in the plural when meaning *thousands of*:
  miles de solicitantes *thousands of applicants*

- cardinals normally precede ordinals:
  los tres primeros pisos *the first three floors*

- Note that the full stop is used with numbers over one thousand and the comma with decimals i.e. the opposite of English usage.

Continued

Ordinal numbers *(first, second, third etc)*

primero (primer, primera)	1°,1ª	undécimo(a)	11°,11ª
segundo(a)	2°,2ª	duodécimo(a)	12°,12ª
tercero (tercer, tercera)	3°,,3ª	decimotercer(o)(a)	13°,13ª
cuarto(a)	4°,4ª	decimocuarto(a)	14°,14ª
quinto(a)	5°,5ª	decimoquinto(a)	15°,15ª
sexto(a)	6°,6ª	decimosexto(a)	16°,16ª
séptimo(a)	7°,7ª	decimoséptimo(a)	17°,17ª
octavo(a)	8°,8ª	decimoctavo(a)	18°,18ª
noveno(a)	9°,9ª	decimonoveno(a)	19°,19ª
décimo(a)	10°,10ª	vigésimo(a)	20°,20ª

Points to note on ordinals

- They agree in gender and in number with the noun, which they normally precede, except with royal titles:

  la primera vez
  the first time

  Felipe segundo
  Philip II

- **primero** and **tercero** drop the **o** before a masculine singular noun:

  el primer premio
  the first prize

  el tercer día
  the third day

- Beyond **décimo** ordinal numbers are rarely used, and they are replaced by the cardinal number placed immediately after the noun:

  el siglo diecisiete
  the seventeenth century

  Alfonso doce
  Alfonso XII

  en el piso trece
  on the 13th floor

  EXCEPTIONS: **vigésimo(a)** 20th (but not with royal titles or centuries)
  centésimo(a) 100th
  milésimo(a) 1,000th
  millonésimo(a) 1,000,000th

Numbers: Other Uses

- collective numbers:

un par	2, a couple
una decena (de personas)	about 10 (people)
una docena (de niños)	(about) a dozen (children)
una quincena (de hombres)	about fifteen (men)
una veintena* (de coches)	about twenty (cars)
un centenar, una centena (de casas)	about a hundred (houses)
cientos/centenares de personas	hundreds of people
un millar (de soldados)	about a thousand (soldiers)
miles/millares de moscas	thousands of flies

*20, 30, 40, 50 can also be converted in the same way.

- measurements:

viente metros cuadrados	20 square metres
veinte metros cúbicos	20 cubic metres
un puente de cuarenta metros de largo/longitud	a bridge 40 metres long

- distance:

De aquí a Madrid hay 400 km	Madrid is 400 km away
a siete km de aquí	7 km from here

Telephone numbers

Póngame con Madrid, el cuatro, cincuenta y ocho, veintidós, noventa y tres
I would like Madrid 458 22 93

Me da Valencia, el viente, cincuenta y uno, setenta y tres
Could you get me Valencia 20 51 73

Extensión tres, tres, cinco/trescientos treinta y cinco
Extension number 335

NB In Spanish telephone numbers may be read out individually, but more frequently they are broken down into groups of two. They are written in groups of two or three numbers (never four).

The Time

¿Qué hora es?	What time is it?
Es ... *(1 o'clock, midnight, noon)*	} *It's ...*
Son las ... *(other times)*	
Es la una y cuarto	*It's 1.15*
Son las diez menos cinco	*It's 9.55*

00.00	**medianoche; las doce (de la noche)**	*midnight, twelve o'clock*
00.10	**las doce y diez (de la noche)**	
00.15	**las doce y cuarto**	
00.30	**las doce y media**	
00.45	**la una menos cuarto**	
01.00	**la una (de la madrugada)** *one a.m., one o'clock in the morning*	
01.10	**la una y diez (de la madrugada)**	
02.45	**las tres menos cuarto**	
07.00	**las siete (de la mañana)**	
07.50	**las ocho menos diez**	
12.00	**mediodía; las doce (de la mañana)** *noon, twelve o'clock*	
13.00	**la una (de la tarde)** *one p.m., one o'clock in the afternoon*	
19.00	**las siete (de la tarde)** *seven p.m., seven o'clock in the evening*	
21.00	**las nueve (de la noche)** *nine p.m., nine o'clock at night*	

NB When referring to a timetable, the 24 hour clock is used:

las dieciséis cuarenta y cinco	16.45
las veintiuna quince	21.15

¿A qué hora vas a venir? — A las siete
What time are you coming? — At seven o'clock

Las oficinas cierran de dos a cuatro
The offices are closed from two until four

Vendré a eso de/hacia las siete y media
I'll come at around 7.30

a las seis y pico
just after 6 o'clock

a las cinco en punto
at 5 o'clock sharp

entre las ocho y las nueve
between 8 and 9 o'clock

Son más de las tres y media
It's after half past three

Hay que estar allí lo más tarde a las diez
You have to be there by ten o'clock at the latest

Tiene para media hora
He'll be half an hour (at it)

Estuvo sin conocimiento durante un cuarto de hora
She was unconscious for a quarter of an hour

Les estoy esperando desde hace una hora/desde las dos
I've been waiting for them for an hour/since two o'clock

Se fueron hace unos minutos
They left a few minutes ago

Lo hice en veinte minutos
I did it in twenty minutes

El tren llega dentro de una hora
The train arrives in an hour('s time)

¿Cuánto (tiempo) dura la película?
How long does the film last?

por la mañana/tarde/noche
in the morning/afternoon or evening/at night

mañana por la mañana	**ayer por la tarde**	
tomorrow morning	yesterday afternoon or evening	
anoche **anteayer**		**pasado mañana**
last night the day before yesterday		the day after tomorrow

Dates

¿Qué día es hoy?	} What's the date today?
¿A qué día estamos?	
Es (el) ...	} It's the ...
Estamos a ...	
uno/primero de mayo	1st of May
dos de mayo	2nd of May
veintiocho de mayo	28th of May
lunes tres de octubre	Monday the 3rd of October
Vienen el siete de marzo	They're coming on the 7th of March

NB Use cardinal numbers for dates. Only for the first of the month can the ordinal number sometimes be used.

Years

Nací en 1970
I was born in 1970
el veinte de enero de mil novecientos setenta
(on) 20th January 1970

Other expressions

en los años cincuenta	during the fifties
en el siglo veinte	in the twentieth century
en mayo	in May
lunes (quince)	Monday (the 15th)
el quince de marzo	on March the 15th
el/los lunes	on Monday/Mondays
dentro de diez días	in 10 days' time
hace diez días	10 days ago

Age

¿Qué edad tiene?	} How old is he/she?
¿Cuántos años tiene?	
Tiene 23 (años)	He/She is 23
Tiene unos 40 años	He/She is around 40
A los 21 años	At the age of 21

INDEX 307

The following index lists comprehensively both grammatical terms and key words in English and Spanish.